MY CRAZIEST
ADVENTURES
WITH
GOD

Volume 2

Jean:

I hope this book blesses you.
Thanks for your friendship!

Prayna Medic

MY CRAZIEST
ADVENTURES
WITH
GOD

Volume 2

*The Spiritual Journal of
a Former Atheist Paramedic*

PRAYING MEDIC

**INKITY
PRESS™**

Inkity Press™
137 East Elliot Road, #2292, Gilbert, AZ 85234

This book and other Inkity Press titles can be found at:
InkityPress.com and PrayingMedic.com/my-books/

Available from Amazon.com, CreateSpace.com, and other retail outlets.

For more information visit our website at **www.inkitypress.com**
or email us at **admin@inkitypress.com** or **admin@prayingmedic.com**

ISBN-13: 978-0692537183 (Inkity Press)
ISBN-10: 069253718X

Printed in the U.S.A.

DEDICATION

I'D LIKE TO DEDICATE THIS book to my friend David McLain, who has been a friend and mentor to me and a companion on my journey into the Kingdom of God.

ACKNOWLEDGMENTS

I'D LIKE TO THANK THE many people who helped in the development of this book by providing feedback on these stories. You know who you are. I greatly value your insights and your encouragement.

I'd like to thank my wife for her time and talents as the cover and interior design artist and for her help with editing the manuscript. I must also say that she is my best friend and without her acknowledgment and support of who God created me to be, many of these stories may never have happened.

I'm grateful to Lydia Blain for her skills and patience as my editor.

~ Praying Medic

NOTE

THE NAMES OF MY PATIENTS have been changed to protect the privacy of their medical information.

TABLE OF CONTENTS

INTRODUCTION

THOSE WHO ARE ACQUAINTED WITH volume one of this series need no introduction, but those who are not will need a little background information about me. When you read these stories, you might think they're the adventures of a well-known healing evangelist or the pastor of a mega-church. Surely, you might think, these things can't happen to average people like me, can they? Believe it or not, these are the true stories of a very average man working an average job, who happens to have a very above average God.

Not long ago, I was an atheist. After becoming a believer, I spent years sitting in a church pew, dozing through sermons and wishing there were more to the Christian life. Then one day I had a conversation with God, who told me that if I wanted to go with Him on a journey outside the four walls of the church, He'd lead me on the adventure of a lifetime. Like a fool, I said yes and my life has never been the same.

As you read these stories, please don't think I'm one of those super-gifted people. I'm not a very gifted person. I'm not a seminary grad or a church super-star. I am however, a bit more adventuresome than the average person. If I had to attribute these stories to any one thing, I would say it was my willingness to do the very thing that seemed most illogical and the one that would make me look like a fool if it didn't work. As the Holy Spirit led, nudged and sometimes demanded that I step out of my comfort zone, I found that a life of miracles was there, waiting for me.

Have you ever noticed that nothing very exciting happens inside your comfort zone? That's because the mojo happens *outside* your comfort zone. And as I told a friend in a dream when she asked me how I get people healed, "It's all about your mojo." Which is to say, it's all about taking a few risks, having a little faith and trusting that God will do something crazy if you step out of your comfort zone.

I didn't write this book for my benefit. I wrote it to encourage and inspire *you*. I want you to know how great God's power is. I want you to know just how far He will go to reach people and how scandalous His love really is. Take note as you read, how He opens doors for me, how He makes divine connections, and how as I take risks, He touches people with His power and love. And realize that whatever He does through me, He will do through you.

~ Praying Medic

No More Shackles

TIMOTHY SAT HUNCHED OVER IN a wheelchair at the entrance to the prison hospital. Wrapped in a white blanket, shivering, pale and emaciated, the long awaited day had finally arrived. He was going home.

The state prison in Florence, Arizona sits like an old fortress atop a hill in the middle of the Sonoran Desert. Outside the city limits are miles of barren land, cacti, and sun-baked reptiles. Not exactly a hospitable environment for a would-be escapee.

We pulled our ambulance up to the main prison gate. There was a newbie at the control panel, who was opening and closing the gates. The guard yelled for him to open one gate and close another, but his orders went unheeded. The confusion would have served us well, if we had plans to break someone out of prison. I was mildly amused when we were allowed inside without passing through the metal detector or being searched. It reminded me of the Apostle Peter's prison break but I didn't see any angels nearby.

Every day the inmates spend hours in the scorching sun, raking every driveway in the prison compound, until all the little white stones lie uniformly next to one another. As we backed the ambulance down the driveway leading to the hospital we left deep tracks in the meticulously raked gravel. We got out, unloaded the gurney and went inside.

The information we had on our patient was sketchy. I asked a guard if he was being released early because he was sick. "Heck, no!" She said with a laugh. "We don't let anyone out before their time is up. If they die here, they die here… and we have plenty of people die in here all the time. Nope, Timothy here served his time and he's being released."

I walked over and introduced myself. Timothy's cracked lips trembled with fear as he stared ahead out the open door of the prison hospital. Tears rolled down his cheeks. Stuttering badly, he tried in vain to form words that made sense. The prison nurse put her arm around him. "What's wrong, Timothy?"

Stammering and stuttering, searching for the right words, he strung together a short phrase. "I don't... want... to be... a burden."

I'd been down this road before with patients who felt their medical problems would be to too burdensome on the ones who would care for them. "Timothy," I said with a smile, "I don't think you're going to be a burden on anyone." I took the nurse aside and asked for all the information she had on him. Timothy was in his early thirties. He had HIV, a brain tumor, and right-side weakness from a stroke which left him unable to speak clearly. He had a feeding tube because he had trouble swallowing and a catheter in his bladder. He was being sent to an unknown destination for hospice care. He wasn't expected to live much longer.

His nurse turned to me. "What facility did you say you're taking him to?"

"That's a good question. We don't have the name of the facility—just an address." I pulled out my phone and called dispatch to ask for the name of the facility, but they didn't have that information.

My partner pulled out his phone and put the address in his mapping program. "It looks like a private residence. There's no business name and it's in a residential neighborhood."

Timothy spoke up. "What's the address?" We told him. After a long pause he smiled. "That's... my... sister's... house."

It was clear now, that he was going to his sister's house and a hospice nurse would meet him there. The likelihood of him being a burden to his family was less than if he were being cared for by someone who didn't know him. I put my hand on his shoulder. "Trust me, after all you've been through, you're not going to be a burden to your family." More tears rolled down his cheek.

We helped him up from the wheelchair and with measured, slow steps he positioned himself to sit on the gurney, his frail frame still draped with the white cotton blanket. The hospital building was well air-conditioned. I was getting cold after being inside for just a few minutes.

"You won't have to worry about being cold, Timothy. It's about 105 degrees outside. Even with the air conditioning on, it'll be 95 degrees in the back of the ambulance." Another smile appeared on his cracked lips. In staccato phrases he asked where his medications were. The nurses looked at one another and shrugged their shoulders. He said he had a bag of medications in his cell and they were supposed to go with him, but no one knew where they were. They told him the prison's policy was to ship out any personal belongings left behind by inmates. He wasn't reassured.

His favorite nurse gave him one more hug before we loaded him up. More tears. She dried his eyes and gave him a few tissues for the road then we put him in the back of the ambulance. Leaving the prison this afternoon was a strange ordeal. Since moving to Arizona, I've transported dozens of inmates. We always have two guards that ride with us, and the inmates are always shackled.

Always. But not today.

We stopped at the first gate and a guard climbed in, clutching a pile of papers. He sat next to me on the bench seat. "This is so weird," the guard said. "There aren't any guards going along. No chase car. No shackles. We never see anyone leave in an ambulance without shackles and a guard."

He gave Timothy a check for $50 and had him sign for it. He explained what the rest of the papers were for and hopped out the back door. The gate in front of us opened, we drove through and it closed. Then we drove a few hundred feet to the next gate. Another guard opened the back door of the ambulance and hopped inside. He took Timothy's yellow Department of Correction ID and gave him a new white ID card. Timothy looked at the picture on his new ID card with disgust, turned to me and said, "Can... we... burn... this?"

We both busted up laughing. He asked the guard about his bag of medications. "We have twelve bags of medications inside, but none of them are yours. I don't know where yours are, but when they turn up, we'll ship them to you." He wished Timothy good luck then disappeared out the back door. The gate opened and we pulled out of the compound onto the main road. My patient was a free man.

Well, sort of.

A few miles down the road, I asked if he had anything special he wanted to eat for his first meal. Words fell from his lips but nothing he said made sense. He couldn't say the name of his favorite burger joint.

"Burger... burger... "

"Burger King?" I asked.

He shook his head.

"McDonald's?"

Wrong again.

"Wendy's?"

Nope.

I rattled off all the burger places I could think of, but missed each time. "Cali... Cali... in and in... "

"In-N-Out?" I asked. A big smile and a nod of agreement. "Are you gonna order off the regular menu or the secret one?"

"Four... by... four," He said, with a grin. The thought of eating a good burger must have put him in a better frame of mind as he told me what was on the legendary "Four by Four." Four beef patties with cheese and all the fixin's. Unfortunately, the nurse clued me in to the fact that he frequently vomits after eating solid food, which is why he had a feeding tube.

"Timothy, what's the hardest part about being in prison?" I assumed it might be the manual labor, the disgusting food, the oppressive heat or fear of what other inmates might do to you.

With a somber look, he started at his feet and said, "Shackles."

Trying his best to form the right words, he explained the feelings that come from being shackled everywhere you go. Whether you're in your cell, in the prison yard, on the bus, in the ambulance or even lying half-dead in a hospital ICU fifty miles from the prison—inmates are never free from the shackles.

"Well, you'll never have to wear shackles again. Today you're a free man." The song *I'll Fly Away* was playing softly in the recesses of my mind. It was about that time when my partner received a call from dispatch telling him they found the missing medications. I broke the news to Timothy.

"It looks like we have to take you back to Florence. But this time, no shackles... they found your medications."

We turned the ambulance around on the dusty road and went back through the first gate. My driver retrieved the bag of pill bottles then we headed out once more. Our destination was 81 miles away. I told Timothy I see a lot of people healed in the ambulance and asked if I could pray with him. He smiled and said yes. I laid my hand on his shoulder and asked God to bless him with peace, confidence, joy, and health. I commanded disease to leave and asked the Holy Spirit to bring His presence. I asked if he felt anything.

"I feel… relief." He said, with a crooked smile.

"Well, I suppose that's better than shackles." I prayed one more time then turned my attention to charting. Timothy rested, gazing out the back window of the ambulance. God only knows what must have been going through his mind. About thirty minutes went by. He slept a little, but was awake again, staring intently and fidgeting.

"What are you thinking about?" I asked. With his eyes still looking out the back window, he slowly explained that he was thinking about how he had lived his life.

"I wanted… to be… a good… example," He stammered. More tears rolled down his cheeks.

I can only imagine how this young man must have viewed his life. What kind of bitterness and disappointment was he feeling? What would it be like to wake up the next morning, knowing you're a free man, trapped inside a life that went terribly wrong?

"Timothy… I was a terrible role model for most of my life. It was only a few years ago that things changed for the better. The doctors I know have a saying: 'You learn how to make good decisions, by making bad decisions.' We all make bad decisions, and God knows I've made my share, but we can learn from them. It's never too late to be a good example to someone."

He smiled, nodded in agreement, wiped away the tears and rested his head, turning his gaze to the back window. An hour later we approached his sister's house. With joy and excitement he told me in the best words he could find when we were going to turn, and which stores we would see. His mother greeted us at the back door of the ambulance. Inside, a house full of relatives waited with excitement. We wheeled the gurney to the back bedroom and I helped him to bed. When he was settled in I when went to the living room and gave report to the hospice nurse. A few minutes later his mother came from the bedroom.

"Timothy wants to see you before you go," she said.

I returned to his bedside. He held out his hand. I gently grasped it and we slowly shook hands as he tried to speak. Stammering and stuttering he said, "Thank you… for being… so nice… to… me."

I bent down and hugged his frail body. With my forehead against his, I said, "You're just awesome, you know that? God loves you and He has a great plan for your future. And if I don't see you in the future, I'll see you in the pasture. And remember… it's never too late to be a good example."

With tears in my eyes, I made my way to the kitchen, left a copy of my report with the nurse and headed for the front door.

The Security Guard

OUR PATIENT WAS A FREQUENT flyer who came to an urgent care facility after a drinking binge. While waiting for the transfer paperwork to be copied, I chatted with the security guard, who told me he was their first patient of the day.

"But, don't you work here?" I asked.

"Yeah… I'm on duty right now, but my bursitis was acting up and I figured they could take a look at it before I went on duty."

They gave him a steroid injection and he put on his uniform. A few hours later we showed up. I asked if he wanted to be healed. He said, "Sure."

Sometimes the need for healing is obvious. Sometimes it isn't. Words of knowledge are great, but often we stumble upon a need for healing in every day conversations. If you spend a few minutes getting to know a stranger they'll probably tell you about their health problems. Once they do, just ask if they want to be healed. After the security guard agreed to let me pray with him, I shared a few testimonies, partly to build his faith and partly to build mine.

"So what's up with your shoulder?" I asked.

"I have a partially torn bicep and a piece of cartilage floating around in the joint. I also have bursitis."

"Sounds messy," I said. I led him around a corner to a vacant hallway for privacy. I placed my hand *lightly* on his injured shoulder (I didn't want to make the pain worse.)

"Holy Spirit, bring your presence and power. Spirit of pain, I command you to leave. Inflammation, get out now. Ligaments, bones, nerves, tendons, muscles and cartilage, I command you to be healed." After a few moments, I asked what he felt.

Grabbing his shoulder, he said, "It's hard to describe. It's like… the pain is gradually leaving."

I touched his shoulder again. "Holy Spirit, bring more of your healing power. Pain and inflammation get out." I asked again what he felt.

The look of amazement on his face turned to a smile. "It's almost completely gone." I asked him to rate his pain on a scale from one to ten. "Maybe a 0.5. I can hardly feel it at all!"

Since symptoms of injury and illness have been known to return, I developed a habit of teaching people how to keep their healing. I told the security guard, "Most people never experience the symptoms again after being healed, but some do. Healing is a battle. There's an enemy who wants you to be in pain and a God who loves you and wants you to be healthy. If the pain comes back, do what I did. Believe that God healed you and command the pain to leave."

Two-For-One Night

MY WIFE AND I HAVE a tradition that we enjoy. After seven years of marriage, we still go on dates. One night we drove to Saguaro Lake, east of Phoenix. On the drive out to the lake we talked about where our future might lead us. Afterward, we went to Chili's restaurant for an appetizer. The food was good, the conversation was light, and the company was beautiful. As we made our way to the exit, my attention was drawn to a young woman wearing a bright red shirt. She happened to be the hostess and she was limping slightly. So guess what I did?

Good guess. I asked if she wanted to be healed. Guess what her reply was. Right again.

Her name was Jill. I introduced myself and my wife and explained that we see people healed at stores and restaurants. "Jill, would you like us to pray for you?"

"I would be delighted."

A second waitress looked on, fascinated by what we were doing. Her name was Stephanie. "Jill and Stephanie, have you ever seen a miracle?" They both said no. "Well, you're about to." Turning to Jill, I asked, "So what's up with your leg?"

"Weird coincidence, actually. About 15 minutes ago I pulled my hamstring and that's why I'm limping."

"How bad is the pain on a scale from one to ten?"

"I'd say about a seven."

"Well then, why don't we get you healed?" I placed my hand on her leg. "Holy Spirit, bring your presence and power." I've never felt His presence show up so quickly. As soon as the words left my mouth we felt the atmosphere change. I began to sway back and forth. "Wow... can you feel that?" I asked my wife, who was nearly on the floor from the weight of God's presence.

I thought about this for a moment. Why did He show up so quickly? It's like He was excitedly waiting for me to say the words, so He could bring His presence into the atmosphere. I believe God is a lot more excited about healing than we are. Standing in the entrance to the restaurant, becoming intoxicated in God's glory, I commanded Jill's hamstring to be healed in the name of Jesus. It took about five seconds for her mouth to drop open in complete shock.

"Oh my God... who are you people? How did you do that?" She was healed immediately and began walking around the restaurant checking out her hamstring. She couldn't believe it happened that fast. She demanded to know how I did it.

I explained: "You know that Jesus went through the cities of Israel healing the sick, raising the dead, casting out demons and proclaiming the kingdom of God don't you? Well if you look in Matthew chapter 10, you'll see that he gave that same authority to his disciples. I'm one of his disciples. Every one of us has this same authority. It's just that most of us have never been taught how to use it."

When you learn to heal the sick and work miracles, it allows you to talk about Jesus. And that's exactly what we did. Jill and Stephanie fired questions at us and we discussed how it all works. They'd seen faith healers on TV, but had never heard of anyone doing healing in public. We told them it's become a lifestyle for us and we explained that anyone can do it. We asked Stephanie if she had anything that needed healing.

"Well, it's nothing big. Just a bone spur on my heel. Maybe you guys can come back some time and pray for me."

"Have a seat and we'll get you healed right now," I replied.

"No, I'm okay. We've already taken enough of your time."

"Sit down," I said with a smile.

Stephanie took a seat. "Here's what I want you to do," I said as I knelt beside her. "I want you to rest your foot on my knee." She lifted her foot up and placed it on my knee. I placed my hand on her foot. "Pain, I command you to leave in the name of Jesus. Bone spur, leave. Foot, be healed right now." I asked if she felt anything.

"It feels weird, like there's a kind of buzzing going on."

Jill chimed in, "That's what I felt, too! It's like this buzzing thing starts and then all the pain is gone!"

"That's the power of God healing you." I asked Stephanie if there was any pain.

"Yes, it still hurts a little."

Once again, I commanded the pain to leave, and then I asked her stand up and check it out. She got up and stomped her foot on the floor repeatedly in amazement. She tried to make the pain come back, but she couldn't. It was gone. We talked some more about Jesus and shared a few healing testimonies and I gave them a crash course on how to keep their healing. Three men walked in the front door and overheard what I said. I told them to ask Jill and Stephanie what just happened to them.

I would imagine they shared their testimonies about Jesus the rest of the night. And that's how the kingdom of God is. When Jesus appears in your life and reveals himself, you're likely to tell everyone you know about the great things He's done for you.

The Kirby Salesman

JONATHON WAS 19 YEARS OLD and living out his dream of being a professional hockey goalie. That dream was shattered when a slap-shot broke his collar bone. Thinking it was just bruised, he stayed in the game. When the bone finally broke completely in two, it severed muscles and tendons and left his shoulder a surgical mess. In the operating room, the surgeons retrieved and reattached the severed sinew, but Jonathon's career as a goalie was over. He pursued a new career as an electrician and did well for himself until the housing market crashed in 2008. As a child, his mother told him, "Be whatever you want to be, just don't grow up to be a Kirby salesman."

One day she received a phone call from her son. Jonathon gently broke the news to her, "Mom, I'm selling Kirby vacuum cleaners." Ten years after the career-ending slap-shot, Jonathon came to our door. He was training new salesmen for Kirby. He introduced us to a young trainee who would demonstrate the wonders of the newest Kirby. When we were all acquainted, Jonathon left. Our salesman, Ryan was excited and full of energy. He began his demonstration and asked if I had a hobby. There was a long pause. I had to think for a minute about what my hobby was. I decided to tell him about healing.

We shared some of our more interesting testimonies and told him about our history with God. He seemed interested and asked a lot of questions. At one point, he became so engrossed in the stories he forgot where he was in his sales presentation and had to check with the outline to get back on track. My daughter, Kelly, watched his sales pitch from the couch. An hour later the doorbell rang. It was Jonathon.

He came in and asked how Ryan was doing. We told him Ryan was doing great, but we couldn't buy the Kirby. He was very understanding.

We talked with Jonathon for a while and he shared his life story with us, including the broken collar bone story. Putting his arm up, he showed us the limited range of motion he still had ten years later. I looked at Ryan.

He looked at me and yelled, "Do it... you gotta do it!"

Ryan had been listening to healing stories for the last hour and now he wanted to see one for himself. Fortunately, Jonathon was a believer. We explained what we'd been talking about and he agreed to let us pray with him. I asked my daughter, "Do you want to do it or should I?"

I didn't give her a choice. I walked to the other side of the living room to watch. My daughter went to his left side and my wife went to his right and they began praying. After 30 seconds we asked Jonathon if he felt anything.

"It feels warm inside and I don't know... there's like this feeling of weightlessness."

I said, "Raise your arms up as high as you can and stop if you feel any pain."

As he raised both arms, we all heard popping noises. He showed full range of motion and touched his hands together above his head. His mouth dropped open. "I haven't been able to do this in ten years!"

We forgot about vacuum cleaners and talked about how much God loves to heal people. Jonathon could not get over his amazement at how easily his healing came. Ryan was just as shocked, because he knew Jonathon couldn't move his arm like that just a few minutes ago. Jonathon said he had degenerative joint disease in his neck and back so we prayed over that and the heat increased. He got a major overhaul.

Seeing Pink

WHILE ARRIVING AT A HOSPITAL with a patient, I noticed a nurse who was limping down the hallway with an immobilizer on her foot. As we passed in the hallway, I told her I wanted to have a word with her after we dropped off our patient. After we got our patient settled in into his room, I went hunting for the nurse. It didn't take long to find her. "Do you mind if I ask why you have the immobilizer?"

"I tore my Achilles tendon and now I have permanent foot drop," She replied. "The immobilizer lets me walk without dragging my foot on the floor."

"What the heck are you doing at work with that kind of injury, shouldn't you be at home?"

"I don't have any paid time off left."

"I see. Well how would you like to be healed?"

She gave me a funny look. "What do you mean healed? Do you use some kind of energy healing?"

"Not exactly," I said. "I pray with people and God heals them." That brought a smile to her face.

"I believe in God and I know He heals people." She agreed to let me pray. I crouched down and put my hand on the immobilizer. "I command this tendon to reattach to the bone right now, in the name of Jesus. Pain and inflammation, leave. Spirit of pain, get out right now!" I asked what she felt.

"It kinda tingles all around my foot."

"Well, that's because God is healing you. Why don't you take the immobilizer off and try walking on it?"

"I can't. If I take it off, I'll get yelled at." She'd seen a specialist who said there was nothing that could be done. She came to work, but had to wear the immobilizer. If a supervisor saw her walking without it, she'd have to explain why. So it was easier for her to leave it on. I encouraged her to trust that she was healed and take it off when she got home.

While all this was happening, a small crowd of nurses had gathered in the hallway. They were curious to know more about how I did this healing, so I shared a few testimonies with them. One woman asked if I used some kind of energy healing.

"Nope. It's all Jesus."

They wanted to know my name and how to contact me. I ran out of business cards, so I wrote my contact information on paper towels. One of the people who saw me praying for the nurse was my new EMT partner. A few days later, at the end of our shift, he brought up the nurse and the healing encounter and asked how I got started in healing. I shared a few healing stories and told him about the many dreams I'd had about healing. "Do most of the people you pray with stay healed, or do their symptoms return?" He asked.

"Most people stay healed, though some have their symptoms return."

"Do you think I could be healed?"

"Absolutely. What's bothering you?"

"Neck pain. I've had it for about three weeks, mostly when I turn my head to the right."

"Do you want to be healed?"

"That would be awesome."

I put my hand on his neck. "Pain, I command you to leave right now in the name of Jesus." I had my eyes closed and saw a faint suggestion of flames. That gave me the impression that God would bring heat to his neck so I went with it. "Lord, increase your heat." I asked what he felt.

"My neck feels pretty warm."

He turned his head left, then right and his mouth dropped open. "That's totally crazy! I can move my head and it doesn't hurt! It's gone!"

We celebrated his miracle. I told Him that God is always looking for people to heal because He loves us so much. The next day we were back at the same hospital. We ran into the nurse I prayed with the day before. She was still wearing the immobilizer.

"How's your foot doing?" I asked.

"It feels great. From the time you prayed for me, there hasn't been any pain." She pointed to the foot immobilizer. "I still have to wear this thing at work so I don't get in trouble, but I have an appointment with my doctor in a few days. I can't wait to hear what he says!"

A co-worker sitting next to her asked if I was the guy she'd been talking about. Apparently there was a lot of talk about healing after I left. This woman wanted to know what type of healing I did. She practices Reiki. I told her my healing comes from Jesus. She was interested in hearing more, so I shared with her some of the things I'd seen God do.

"Would you pray for me? I have three bad heart valves and emphysema."

"Of course I'll pray for you."

I knelt beside her. "Holy Spirit, bring your presence and touch this daughter of yours. Heart valves, I command you to be healed in the name of Jesus." I asked if she felt any different.

"It's the weirdest thing... I feel like there are butterflies in my heart. There's this wonderful fluttering feeling. And I can see the color pink."

Recently, I had been seeing the color pink, too. "Sometimes I see the color pink, especially when I'm praying and I say certain words, like "life," "healing" and "power." I see pink lights that glow brightly, which is how the Holy Spirit tells me that my words carry healing power." Not only did she feel as if her heart was being healed, but she felt like she could breathe better. We talked about healing for another fifteen minutes. She hugged me and thanked me for praying with her. I told her I'd be back for a follow-up report.

God can connect you to people who need healing through a testimony. When one person is healed—and they testify about it—their testimony encourages others to find you, if they want to be healed.

Wonderfully Jaded

A WARM BREEZE WHISTLED THROUGH the junipers as Jade made her way down through the canyons on the long drive from Flagstaff to Phoenix. Todd ran his fingers through his girlfriend's coal-black hair and smiled at her. Jade checked her blind spot and maneuvered the car left to pass slower traffic. As she accelerated, she glanced at Todd and squeezed his hand in hers.

Eyes focused on the road ahead, she noticed that her lane was ending and she had not yet passed all the cars that were in front of her. She could not move right without hitting another car. As her wheels went into the soft gravel on the shoulder, her foot went for the brake pedal and she cut the steering wheel hard to the right to stay on the road. The car slid sideways and for a moment, the tires screeched, then everything became silent as the car became airborne. It came down hard on the roadway and shattered the car's windows, then bounced off the pavement and rolled until it came to rest in the median leaving a trail of books and papers scattered on the freeway.

Todd crawled from the wreckage and began searching the tall grass in the median for his girlfriend. Panicked at the thought of what he might find, he ran as quickly as his injured leg would allow. The smell of fresh blood filled his nostrils and there before him, lay the battered and broken body of his girlfriend, Jade. He gently cradled her blood-soaked head in his hands. "Don't move honey. You're hurt really bad. Just stay still. The ambulance is on its way."

The sensations of pain gradually faded until she felt only a deep sense of peace and freedom like she had never know before. After pausing for a moment to rest, she got up from the grass. Looking at the freeway, then at the brilliant light to her left, and finally down at her body, still lying motionless in the grass, she said, "Come on Jade. Let's get going. We gotta get to Phoenix. It's getting cold out here. We better get moving."

Jade walked along the edge of the road for a few hundred feet then looked back again at her body, still lying motionless in the grass. "Come on Jade, let's go. Phoenix is this way."

Four weeks later...

Jade wheeled herself down the hallway of the nursing home. Two men in blue uniforms approached with a gurney. The taller one made eye contact and she quickly averted her gaze from him as they passed. She reached the nurse's station when the taller paramedic said to the nurse outside her room, "We're looking for Jade. Have you seen her?"

"That's me," she hollered down the hallway. "I'm almost ready to go. Meet me outside the day room. I gotta take my pain meds."

From the moment I saw Jade I had a feeling she was our patient. The first thing I noticed was that her jaw was wired shut. Not completely shut. She could still talk, though she had a limited ability to open her mouth. Bright orange spacers stuck out between her lips where her teeth were dislodged. Dark blue circles around her eyes and a plastic tracheostomy tube sticking out of her neck gave her an almost comic-book like appearance.

I was deeply bothered by the fact that she wouldn't look me in the eye when she saw us coming toward her. I sensed that she was terribly ashamed of how she looked. I felt that if God opened a door for me to pray with her, that's one of the things He would have me address. Jade asked a nurse for her medications while I got report. As the charge nurse told me her story, I flipped through the packet of paperwork to make sure nothing was missing. Jade had finished taking her pills and was ready to go. "What's the best way to get you on the gurney?" I asked.

"If you give me your hand to hold onto I can do it myself," she said. The wires and spacers caused a little difficulty speaking, but it was easy enough to understand her. It was obvious she wanted as much independence as she could get, and I wasn't going to stand in her way. I put out my hand and she grabbed it then lifted herself out of the wheelchair. Standing on one leg she pivoted onto the gurney.

"Do you want me to help get your legs up?" I asked.

"No, I can do it myself."

She swung her left leg up then the right one, which had a full length immobilizer on it. As I buckled the seat belt across her legs I noted the long surgical scar starting just below her knee and ending just above her ankle. I introduced myself and my partner, and we headed toward the elevator.

We were taking Jade to a follow-up appointment to find out if she could have the wires in her jaw removed. I got my computer fired up and began entering her information in my report. After we loaded Jade in the ambulance, I got a set of vital signs, entered them in my computer, and wrote up a quick summary of the transport. I wanted to get the report done as quickly as possible so I might have some time to talk with her.

"Hey Jade... I have a question for you. Are you having any pain right now?"

"Not really."

"Are you serious?"

"Yeah, why?"

"Well, because you look like you should be having pain somewhere."

"Well, I really don't have any pain right now."

"Okay. I have another question. When was your accident?"

"Four weeks ago. I'll never forget it. I was driving down from Flagstaff to Phoenix with my boyfriend Todd. I went to pass a car and I lost control. The car was totaled. I lost eight units of blood on scene and I died for nine minutes."

"No kidding," I said absent-mindedly. "Hey Jade... I have a kind of hobby. I collect stories from people who have had near-death experiences. Do you remember anything from when you died?"

"Yeah. I remember laying in the grass in the median and my boyfriend was looking for me. He found me and told me I was hurt pretty badly. Then I got up and I saw a really bright light. It was like a field of snow. I don't like cold and snow so I looked at myself lying on the ground and said, 'Come on Jade we gotta get to Phoenix. It's this way. It's cold here. Let's get going.' The next thing I remember I was in the hospital."

"Okay, thanks. I have another question... can I pray for you?"

"Yes! Of course you can."

"Cool. But I need to ask you another question first. When you met me in the hallway, you wouldn't look at me. Why did you look down at the floor?" Her chatty demeanor suddenly grew silent. She pulled out her phone and began flipping through a gallery of pictures. When she got to one she liked she held her phone up so I could see it better. Looking at the poses in the pictures, I could tell she had done some modeling before the accident.

"You don't understand. I used to be beautiful. And now... I look like this."

Her self-esteem had been destroyed by the injuries to her face. "Jade, you will always be beautiful because true beauty is who you are on the inside. I think you're an awesome person. But I believe God wants to heal your injuries and make your face look the way it did before the accident. So I'm gonna pray now."

I placed my hand on her cheekbone. "Holy Spirit, do what you do best. Make all things new. I command these bones to be healed. I command the muscles to be healed. Ligaments and tendons, be healed right now. All connective tissue, be healed. I command this eye to be made whole in the name of Jesus." I asked what she felt.

"Tingling."

"Where?"

Pointing to the area near her cheek she said, "Right here. It feels weird."

"That's the power of God healing you."

"You really think He'll heal me?" She asked hopefully.

"I know He wants you to be healed."

"Will you pray for my jaw too?"

"Sure thing." I placed my hand near her chin, but not touching it. "I command these bones to be healed and aligned according to God's perfect plan. I command all deformity to be removed. Soft tissues, be healed. Fractures, be healed. Nothing missing, nothing broken. Lord, I thank you for your healing power." I asked again what she felt.

"Now my jaw is tingling," she said with a smile.

"Sweet! Well, it looks like God is on the case. I wonder what your face will look like tomorrow morning."

We chatted the rest of the trip and I shared a few healing stories with her. She called her dad and told him I prayed for her. "He's going to meet us there," she informed me.

Well that should be fun, I thought to myself. I assumed he was a believer, but I was a little concerned that maybe he wasn't. We arrived and unloaded the gurney. Jade had an unusual request. She didn't want us to take her inside on the gurney. She was too embarrassed, so she asked if we would let her go inside in her wheelchair, which she asked us to bring along. I wasn't in a mood to argue and I admired her independence. "Yeah, no problem," I said. "We'll help you into your wheelchair."

After she got situated, we wheeled her inside. We escorted her to the top floor of the medical building, then located the doctor's office and got her registered. We were escorted to a corner office that had a breathtaking view of downtown Phoenix. It was then that I realized I had forgotten her paperwork in the ambulance.

I left Jade with my partner and went back to the elevators. Several elevators opened at once and a crowd of people began moving past me, each person looking for a particular office. I noticed a man and a woman in their forties looking at the signs for the numbered offices. The Holy Spirit nudged me in their direction.

"Are you looking for Jade?" I asked.

The man drew near with a welcome smile. "Yes, we are." He reached out to shake my hand.

I shook his hand. "Hi, I'm the medic that brought your daughter here."

"Yes, she told us about you. Thank you for praying for her."

"Yeah, no worries. It was my pleasure. She's in the last suite at the end of the hall on the right. I have to go the ambulance. I'll be back in a flash." I went to the ambulance, retrieved the transfer packet and returned to the office. The envelope included all of her records and three CDs worth of medical images, including a couple of x-rays and a CT scan. The doctor would need them in order to evaluate the progress of her healing.

I joined Jade and her parents in the exam room and we got acquainted. As they spoke with her about what she could expect with her first appointment, I could tell they were very supportive parents. I sat in my chair gazing out the window at the skyscrapers towering over the blanket of palm trees. My mind anticipated the inevitable conversation I was about to witness between Jade and the surgeon. He was going to tell her not to get her hopes up. "You're going to take a long time to heal. You're never going to do this again, and you'll probably never do that again…" it would be the same negative crap they always tell their patients. So I decided to make a preemptive strike.

"Jade, when the doctor comes in, he's going to tell you his opinion about your chances for a full recovery. You won't like what he's going to say. He's going to paint a pretty bleak picture. It's how they're trained. They don't want to give people false hope. So when he says, 'You'll never do this or that again,' just nod your head and smile… and know in your heart that God has a different plan for you. Ask the doctor whatever questions you want, but don't let his answers rob you of hope. I've seen so many miracles over the years, it's crazy. A doctor will tell someone they'll never walk again and a year later, they're walking. A doc will tell someone they'll never hike a mountain again and six month later, after they're healed, they're out hiking again. Jade, God wants to heal you. Don't ever forget that."

Her father was all smiles. I could tell he was waiting for a chance to add his views to the conversation, so I let him take over. He reiterated everything I said and encouraged her to keep believing that God would heal her injuries.

A few minutes later the doctor came in. He introduced himself and explained what he wanted to accomplish during the exam. He said he was part of a team of people who would be working with her during the process of rehabilitation. He gave her the names of the other team members and outlined a schedule of appointments she would have over the next few months with different specialists. Then he asked what it was she wanted today.

"I want to know if you can take the wires out of my jaw."

"Well Jade, that all depends on what kind of wires we're dealing with. I'll have to look at the films and see what kind of appliances they used during the surgery." Looking at me he asked, "Did you bring the CDs?"

"We sure did. The receptionist has them."

"Okay, let me have a look at the films and I'll be right back with an answer." When he left, a silence fell upon the room.

"Hey Jade, how does your chin feel?" I asked trying to encourage her.

"Still tingling," she said, smiling through the orange spacers. The doctor returned a few minutes later.

"Jade, I'm sorry, but the kind of appliance they put in can't be removed today in the office. It's screwed into your jaw and it would be too painful to take out in the office. You're going to have to be asleep when we take it out, so you'll have to schedule an appointment for surgery." A look of disappointment appeared on her face. "What other questions do you have for me?"

"Am I ever going to look like I did before?"

He picked up a human skull model off the desk. "Jade, let me explain exactly what we're up against. Your lower jaw was broken into five pieces that are now wired together." Pointing to the areas of the jaw that were fractured, he said, "there's one piece here, one here, another here, one here, and a little piece on this side. Your upper jaw was broken into several pieces as well," He continued, "Here, here and here." Turning the skull around he pointed to the rear of the skull near the base, "You have another fracture at the back of your skull here," turning it one more time he continued, "The zygomatic arch, that's the bone that forms your cheek, was fractured too. There's a metal plate screwed into it to hold it in place. Eventually the plate will come out. The floor of your eye socket was also fractured, which is why your eye is drooping on that side. We'll show you some exercises you can do to help correct that. The base of your skull near the front and a few bones of your mid-face were also fractured. The biggest problem we're going to have is trying to get all these broken pieces to line up again. Before your jaw was fractured, the upper and lower jaws lined up as they were meant to, but now that we have all these broken pieces wired back together, it's going to be almost impossible to make them take the same shape and alignment they had before. All of that means that it's hard to tell exactly what your face will look like a year from now. Re-modeling takes time, and we can do some work to try to reconstruct things if we have pictures to work with, but I can't make any promises."

Listening to him describe the fractures and what they had to do to put everything back together, I was amazed that she survived. Jade pulled out her phone and began showing him the dozens of photos that were taken of her face when she was doing modeling.

"Okay, those will help a lot. Just send them to us and we'll put them in your file."

And with that, the appointment came to an abrupt end. The doctor thanked Jade and her parents for coming and shook their hands before leaving. Her parents thanked me for taking an interest in Jade. We filed out of the room and made our way to the elevator. Jade had to use the bathroom so we stopped in the hallway and waited for her.

Her father looked at me and said, "I have a question for you, if you don't mind my asking."

"I don't mind at all. What's on your mind?"

"I have this pain, right about here," he said, pointing to a spot just below his ribcage.

"Want me to pray for you?" I asked.

"That would be great."

I placed my hand on the spot he indicated. In a barely audible voice I said, "Lord, bring your power and presence upon this man. I command spirits of pain to leave in Jesus' name. I command all inflammation to leave right now." I asked how he felt.

"Better, thanks!"

He pulled a business card from his pocket and handed it to me. "I specialize in physical training and exercise. If you ever need my services, give me a call. I'd be glad to help you in any way I can."

Jade wheeled herself out of the bathroom. "Ready to go?"

"Yup," I said. "Let's get this show on the road."

We wheeled her to the elevator, then to the ambulance and got her loaded for the return trip. On the way back we talked about what her future might look like.

"Jade, it's going to be alright. God is going to heal you."

"Can you pay over my jaw again?"

"I'd love to."

I prayed, Jade wept, and Jesus sat between us smiling. In the dim light of the ambulance I could almost see Him holding her face in his nail-scarred hands.

Giving Thanks

ON THE WAY HOME FROM work one day, I stopped at a store to pick up marshmallows and chocolate bars to make s'mores. The recent spell of cool weather had drawn us outside around the fire pit in the evenings. On the day before Thanksgiving, the store was crowded. A few minutes after I arrived, I saw a woman in front of me reaching for a gallon of milk. She had an immobilizer on her right wrist.

"Excuse me… are you in a hurry?" I asked.

"Yes, I am," she replied.

"Do you happen to have carpal tunnel syndrome?"

She looked at her wrist. "I haven't had it diagnosed yet, but my thumb hurts constantly and I have this weird buzzing sensation in my wrist when I move it."

I introduced myself, told her I was a paramedic, and that I've prayed with a lot of my patients who have been healed. "If you'd like to be healed, I'd be happy to pray for you."

"Gosh, I would just love that," she gushed.

I asked her to hold out her hand and as she did, I gently placed my fingertips on her hand. "Pain and inflammation, I command you to leave right now." I asked if she felt anything.

Her first response was "no" but then a moment later, she said, "It feels warm."

"That's the power of God healing you."

"Is this a Christian thing?" She asked.

"You probably know that Jesus went around healing a lot of people, right? Well, he gave authority to his disciples to do the same thing and that's what I'm doing. I'm one of His disciples and I believe He's healing you."

"Oh, thank you!"

Some people are offended when you tell them you're a Christian, but some are grateful. I asked her to hold out her hand again and when she did, I placed my hand on hers. "I command the spirit of pain to leave in the name of Jesus. Muscles, ligaments, tendons, nerves and bones, be made whole. How do you feel?"

Looking at her hand with a smile, she said. "It doesn't hurt anymore." I asked if there was any pain at all. "Not even a little bit. It seems to be healed." She looked at me and said, "You know... this is so weird. This is the third time in a year that a complete stranger has walked up to me in a store and told me about God."

I smiled. "I guess God has you on His radar. He's going to do some amazing things with you."

She asked if I thought she could be healed of multiple sclerosis and fibromyalgia. I told her a story about a woman at Walmart with MS who was ready to get out of her wheelchair when we were done praying. Her hope began to soar. I asked where she lived. Her home was just a few miles from us, so I wrote my phone number on the back of a business card and told her we would be happy to meet with her for more prayer.

A stranger might tell you they're in a hurry. But when a hungry soul sees that the meal you're serving is the power and love of God, they'll make time for it. And when they receive it, they'll have one more reason to be thankful.

The Chaplain

EARLY ONE MORNING, I SAW a middle-aged hospital chaplain walking through a deserted hospital corridor. I couldn't help but smile when I saw him. His arm was in a sling. I walked toward him and stretched out my hand. "I see I might be too late." His right arm was in a sling and he carried a pile of books in his left hand. We shook hands awkwardly.

"I was going to ask if I could pray with you, but if you already had surgery, maybe you don't need to be healed. I've been praying with my patients and I've seen a lot of them healed."

"Really?" He replied. "Well, God must have given you a gift."

I smiled. "It's not really a gift. Although there is a gift of healing mentioned in the Bible, healing miracles are available to every disciple of Jesus. He gave His disciples authority and power to heal. I've just learned how to operate in it, but anyone can do it. So can I ask what happened to your shoulder?"

"I had surgery and it didn't go well. There wasn't much they could do to repair it. I already have back pain from a bulging disc and knee pain from the spill I took on my mountain bike. The last thing I really needed was more bad news. This shoulder problem could end my career."

We discussed healing and I shared a few testimonies with him. In the end, we both wanted the same thing. I wanted someone to pray with and he wanted to be healed. With a look of hope, he asked, "If you don't mind, would you pray for my knee?"

"I'd love to," I said, as a fire department crew walked through the hallway with a patient on a gurney. A young woman with them looked at me, started laughing, and said, "I know what you're doing!"

I looked at the chaplain. "That's my partner. Holy Spirit, bring your presence." I felt the atmosphere change and I placed my hand on his knee. "Spirit of pain I command you to leave. Cartilage, ligaments, bone, nerves, tendons, blood vessels and muscles, I command you to be healed. All things made brand new, because God doesn't recycle. He makes everything new." I asked if he felt anything different.

He squatted down and flexed his knees. "Not really."

"Sometimes healing can take 10 or 15 minutes, sometimes an hour or two and sometimes even a day or two. Let me pray again." I placed my hand on his knee again. "Pain and inflammation, leave now, in Jesus name." I asked if he felt anything yet.

With a smile, he said, "I'm feeling something happening in there now. Would you mind praying for my back?"

I placed my hand on his lower back. I repeated the same process I used for his knee. After the third time, he said, "Now I'm feeling heat in my back."

"That's the power of God healing you."

"I'm almost afraid to ask you to pray for my shoulder. The doc said it's bone-on-bone. I'm eventually going to need another surgery to replace the joint."

"Why don't we have God replace it right now?" I placed my hand on the injured shoulder. "I command the spirit of pain to leave and the bones, muscle, cartilage, ligaments, tendons, nerves, blood vessels and all the structures of the shoulder to be healed, right now in Jesus' name. How does it feel?"

"It's getting warm."

I repeated the process two more times and asked what was happening.

"I feel a lot of heat now."

"I'd imagine that shoulder will feel pretty good in a couple of hours."

"You know, if you took this far enough, you might put the hospital out of business."

I had to get back to work. I thanked him for his time and went looking for my partner. "Put the hospital out of business," I said to myself. "That's a good one."

Time Warp

My wife drives me to work every day. We have a morning routine that involves snooze alarms, two types of coffee, and an ingenious method of getting hot water from our garage to our bathroom. When I turn on the water to take a shower in the morning nothing but cold water comes out. For some reason it takes an eternity to get warm water to the shower, which is separate from the bathtub. I discovered that if I turn on the hot water in the tub and let it run for a few minutes while the water is running in the shower, it helps purge out the cold water. Since I prefer a medium roast, while my wife likes dark roast coffee, I make my coffee while the water is running and after I'm through with my shower, I make coffee for my wife. One day we left the house at 5:43 am. It was a little later than I like to leave, but it should have put us at the station at 6:00 am, the exact time that my shift starts.

We had been driving for about ten minutes, when I looked at the clock on the dash of the car. The time it showed indicated we had left the house just four minutes ago. I pulled my phone out of my pocket to check the time, thinking maybe the clock in the car was wrong, but it showed the same time: 5:47 am. Only four minutes had passed since we left the house. Even in light traffic, with solid green lights, there's no way we could have driven the distance we covered in just four minutes. I couldn't understand why the time was wrong, but I didn't want to obsess over it, so I put it out of my mind. My wife and I talked about the dreams we had the night before and we arrived at the station at 5:54 am: six minutes early. I clocked in and helped my partner check off the gear.

A crew that was coming off duty at 6:00 am came over and asked if we were going "in service" soon. Dispatch wanted them to take a call and if they did, it would make them late. The EMT wanted to go home because he planned on driving his daughter to her first day of school. I told him we'd be happy to take the call for them. We put our gear on the ambulance and went in service two minutes before our start time of 6:00 am. The EMT thanked me repeatedly for taking the call. We got the call information and went en route. To me, it was just another call.

Twelve hours later, at the end of our shift, the same crew came on duty again. The EMT met me at the time clock and repeatedly thanked me for taking the call for him that morning. His daughter was glad that he was able to take her to school. He made a big deal about it, but to me, it wasn't worth making a fuss over. And yet there was this nagging question in the back of mind... how did I manage to arrive at work six minutes early after leaving the house late? And why?

I've been interested in learning about how God alters time. Or rather, how He alters our perception of it. I've listened to testimonies about time alteration with curiosity. To my knowledge, it had never happened to me before. I've listened to theories about how it happens, but I don't think I could explain the process itself.

If I had not arrived six minutes early for shift change, the EMT would have had no choice but to go on the call and he would not have been able to take his daughter to her first day of school. I found out a few days later that his daughter suffered severe separation anxiety and going to school without her dad on the first day would have caused her to have terrible anxiety. In the eyes of God, it was worth getting me to work six minutes early to spare a little girl that trouble. If what I experienced truly was God altering time, it wasn't for my own gain, my convenience, or my amusement. It happened because God wanted to bless someone else. John Paul Jackson said, "The entire population of the earth, with one very small exception, is comprised of others." Maybe God releases these supernatural events because He wants to bless all those "others" through us.

The Guitar Player

WE FOUND TOM IN THE emergency department screaming in pain. He's a guitar picker by night and he works a manufacturing job by day. He was moving a large sheet of Plexiglas several inches thick, weighing close to 500 pounds, when it crashed to the ground on top of his fingers. Whether or not he'll play guitar again remains to be seen.

The report I got from the nurse said the index and middle fingers on his right hand were completely crushed. I think the term she used was "filleted." They wrapped his hand, started IV antibiotics, gave him some Dilaudid and called us. He was being transferred to a trauma center for surgery to repair what was left of his picking fingers. Pain control wasn't the only thing on his mind.

"Well, at least it's not my fretting hand," he joked. I told him he could learn to use the other fingers to hold the pick. He agreed, but then he said, "Hey look, I'm 30 years old. Maybe my best playing days are behind me."

"I'm twenty years older than you and I'm just beginning my guitar lessons." I replied. (And besides, if he didn't get healed of something, this would just be another depressing, forgettable story.) I reviewed his medical information and asked what medications he took. He gave me the names of three blood pressure pills then added, "... and I take Vicodin and Soma."

Vicodin is a narcotic pain reliever and Soma is a muscle relaxer. This combination is frequently used to treat chronic back pain and chronic pain is something I have a lot of faith to see healed. This information was almost as good as a word of knowledge.

"What are you taking them for?"

"I have back pain all the time."

I couldn't help but smile. I wasn't glad that he had back pain. I was glad he had something I had faith for. I've never seen smashed fingers healed yet, but I've seen a lot of back injuries healed. I knew if we could get his back healed, we had a shot at getting his fingers healed.

With people who have multiple problems, I try to start with the one I have the most experience with. I often ask people if they have a headache and if they say yes, I command it to leave repeatedly until it's gone. Obtaining victory over one thing demonstrates to you and to them that God is willing to heal them. After one thing is healed, you can move to the next thing, getting one condition healed at a time, starting with the one you have the most faith for.

"Hey, Tom, tell me what you know about your back pain."

"I pretty much live with pain every day. The MRI says I have bulging L4 and L5 discs. My doctor wants to do surgery, but I keep putting it off because I really don't want to go through with it." As I talked with him, I decided to try a slightly different approach for getting him healed. I usually command back pain to leave, but this time I was curious to know if he could be healed just by God's presence and a few healing testimonies.

I invited the Holy Spirit to bring His presence into the ambulance and talked with him about people I've seen healed in the past. I placed my hand on his hip then shared a dream I had about a man with severe crushing injuries who was healed by the presence of God, without me praying for him. He said it would be cool if something like that happened to him.

After telling him about the dream, I asked how his back was feeling. His eyes grew as large as saucers. "Now you're creeping me out!" He shouted. "Hey, I can't feel any pain in my back!"

"Why don't you move around a little to make sure?" He twisted in both directions, but there was no pain. It was completely gone. Knowing that his back was healed, my faith began to rise.

"How bad is the pain in your hand?"

"It hurts like crazy."

I placed my hand so that I was barely touching the gauze bandages. "Spirit of pain, I command you to leave. Blood vessels, nerves, bones, tendons and muscles, be healed in the name of Jesus." I asked how his hand felt.

"There was a really bad, burning pain going all the way through my hand, but it's not as bad now."

I prayed again and asked how bad the pain was.

"It's a lot less now. You know… I think I could almost go to sleep."

"You can rest if you want, Tom. I don't have any more questions to ask you. I believe that when the surgeon takes these bandages off, your fingers are going to be as good as new. Why don't you sleep for the rest of the trip?"

Tom was in excruciating pain when we picked him up. He was anxious about the possibility of never playing guitar again, and wondering when he'd have to go under the knife for back surgery. Twenty minutes later, he was resting in the peaceful presence of God. I'm pretty sure I have the coolest job in the world.

Ortho Appointment

VANESSA SAT ON THE GURNEY as the doctor examined her. He asked her questions while testing her ability to flex and extend her feet. Her tracheostomy made it hard to hear the answers. Her words came out in a muffled whisper. It was easier to read her lips.

Vanessa was being seen several months after a car accident, which left her severely disabled and in a lot of pain. She'd been brought to an orthopedic appointment by another crew that had been held past the end of their shift and they needed to go home. We were taking over patient care from them. The medic who was taking care of her gave me a quick report then headed for her ambulance. The doctor finished his exam. Before leaving the exam room, he told Vanessa he'd be praying for her. I love it when doctors pray for their patients. (Now if we can just teach them how to get them healed.)

I introduced myself and Vanessa whispered her story to me. I already knew a few details, having listened during the exam. She'd been in a car accident that left her with a lot of broken bones in her arms and legs. She also had airway problems that required a tracheostomy. Vanessa rubbed her left wrist.

"Does your wrist hurt?" I asked.

"Yes," she whispered.

"On a scale from one to ten how bad is it?"

"About a six."

Both wrists hurt, but the left was worse than the right. "Can I pray with you?"

She whispered, "Sure. I pray every day."

I couldn't help but notice the surgical scars on her wrists where pins, plates and screws had been inserted to hold the broken bones in place. "Alright Jesus, you like healing people, so let's get her healed. Holy Spirit, bring your presence and touch her. I command pain and inflammation to leave, evil spirits to leave. Muscles, ligaments, bones, tendons, nerves and cartilage, I command you to be healed now in the name of Jesus." I asked what she felt.

She moved her hands in circles, smiled and said, "Nothing."

"What do you mean by 'nothing'?"

"No pain. They feel great," she whispered as she continued rotating her wrists to make sure she wasn't imagining it.

"Is there any pain at all?"

"Maybe just a little in the left one."

By now my partner was getting involved. Having been healed of neck pain two weeks earlier and seeing a few patients healed since then, he told Vanessa she would be healed too. I prayed over her left wrist a second time and the pain vanished. "Now let's get your feet healed."

I asked how much pain she had in her feet and checked her range of motion. The atrophy in her right leg was the greatest concern. Her left calf was twice the size of her right one and she had a limited ability to move her right foot. Her ankles hurt constantly. "You won't have any pain when I'm done." I had to believe that if God healed her wrists, He would heal her feet. "I command pain and inflammation to leave, spirits of pain, get out! Muscles, ligaments, bones, tendons, nerves and cartilage, I command you to be healed." I asked how her feet felt.

Smiling, she said, "They feel great. All the pain is gone." That's when the doctor returned. I told him what we'd been up to. He seemed pleased by her testimony and remarked that God's ways are wonderful and mysterious. On the trip back to the nursing home, I asked if she wanted me to pray for her throat to be healed so they could remove her tracheostomy tube.

"I'd love that."

I placed my hand on her arm. "Swelling and soft tissue damage, I command you to leave. I release the healing power of the kingdom of heaven." I asked once more what she felt.

"There's heat going into my arm. It's coming out of your hand."

I gave Vanessa a quick lesson on how to keep her healing before we arrived at the nursing home. God does His part, when we do our part. And our part is to believe that He'll do what He's done in the past.

On Target

MY DAUGHTER AND I HAVE a Saturday morning ritual. We check what's left in the pantry and refrigerator then make a pilgrimage to Costco to restock. On the way home, we always stop at a second store to get a few things we can't get at Costco. This Saturday we stopped at Target. We were cruising the aisles when my daughter said, "Hey dad, did you see the lady with the leg immobilizer?" I was too busy looking for things on my list and hadn't noticed her. After a few minutes of searching, we found her in the refrigerated food aisle. I could tell that my daughter wanted to see her healed, so I walked up and asked how she injured her foot.

"I tore my Achilles tendon."

"How did it happen?"

"It's one of the rare side-effects you can get from taking Levaquin."

"I've never heard of an antibiotic causing something like a torn tendon. Did you have surgery to repair it?

"Not yet. I'm scheduled for surgery in two weeks."

I would have already introduced myself, but Lori was so friendly and willing to discuss her life with a couple of strangers, I decided to wait and let her tell us as much as she wanted, without telling her who we were and what we were up to. I like building bridges of trust before asking if I can pray with someone, and this bridge was going up quickly. When it was time for introductions, I told her my name and introduced my daughter. I thought it would be good to share one testimony before we asked if she wanted to be healed, so I told her the story about an EMT who had his torn Achilles tendon healed at work.

"So Lori, would you like to be healed?

"I sure would."

My daughter and I placed our hands on her immobilized ankle. I asked the Holy Spirit to bring His presence and touch her. I don't know if she felt His presence, but I certainly did. My daughter commanded pain, inflammation, and spirits of infirmity to leave. We asked if she felt anything.

"It feels hot down there."

"Awesome. That's the power of God healing you." We prayed a second time. "Tendon, I command you to reattach to the heel bone in the name of Jesus." I asked what she felt.

"I feel a pulling sensation near my heel."

"What you're feeling might be your Achilles tendon reattaching to your heel bone. You may want to remove the immobilizer and try to walk without it when you get home." We spent a few more minutes talking. She thanked us repeatedly for stopping to pray with her. I told her how to find my website and asked her to drop us an e-mail and let us know how she was doing.

My daughter gave me a high five as we walked away...

and a fist bump.

Adopting Monica

EN ROUTE TO THE CALL, I pulled out my phone and searched the internet for the diagnosis we got from dispatch. I'd never heard of NDMA encephalopathy. Wikipedia said it's a rare autoimmune disease, typically affecting young women, often associated with ovarian tumors. The onset is usually gradual, with altered mental status, seizures, and eventually coma. The long term prognosis is good, if the patient is properly diagnosed and treated.

We arrived at the ICU to find Monica lying in bed. The first thing I noticed was that her facial muscles were in a constant state of twitching. The second was that she was unable to respond to me. Her father and mother introduced themselves and began telling me about her condition. Monica's father is a paramedic instructor from a small town in Texas. They brought her to Mayo hospital in Phoenix because it's one of the only hospitals in the Southwest with the ability to diagnose and treat her condition.

As I shook hands with her mother, I couldn't help but notice the beautiful necklace draped around her neck. Dangling from the necklace was a gold cross. As people wandered in and out of the room, her nurse gave me report. From an envelope, she pulled a stack of papers that were stapled together and handed them to me. "Here," she said, "You need to give these to the people who will be taking care of her where she's going".

"Uh, okay. Can I ask what these papers are?"

"Sure. This is going to sound a little weird, but for the past four months, all of us nurses who have been taking care of Monica have been recording everything she's gone through. Every shift we've taken turns writing notes on her progress. We put everything into a journal that has to stay with her."

The stack of papers was not part of her hospital medical records. It was a collective, personal journal the nurses decided to do on their own. As I read the notes, I smiled. They recorded all of her procedures, every seizure she had and every change in mental status. I noticed that Monica's finger nails were painted. The nail polish looked fresh. An attractive pink stripe pattern adorned each nail, except for the middle finger on her left hand, which was bare. "Who did her nails?" I asked.

"We all did!" One of the nurses replied. The room had quickly filled with nurses, techs, and other employees who wanted to see Monica off. "I see you left one finger without polish... nice touch."

"Of course! That's for the pulse ox probe."

Thick nail polish can impede the pulse oximetry sensor, which makes those annoying alarms go off. So it's wise to remove the nail polish on one finger. They thought of everything. I can't recall ever seeing a group of nurses who became so involved in the personal life of a patient. It was like they'd adopted her as a sister.

We carefully moved Monica to the gurney and got her covered and belted in for the trip. The loving people from Mayo bade her farewell as we rolled her to the elevator. Her mother was riding with us. Inside the ambulance, I asked if I could pray for her daughter. "By all means, please do!" She replied.

I closed my eyes, placed my hand on her shoulder, and declared life over her. I immediately saw in my mind's eye, Monica sitting up with her eyes open, talking to her mother as if nothing was wrong. I commanded sickness to leave and for her immune system to be healed. We both prayed for this lively young woman who was trapped in a broken body.

"Can I tell you what I saw when I was praying?" I asked.

"Of course you can. I'd be very interested in hearing what you saw."

"As I prayed, in my mind's eye, God showed me a vision of Monica. She was sitting up on the gurney talking to you like there was nothing wrong with her. I think it means that she's aware of what's going on around her." I shared with her some of the visions I've seen during prayer and a few of the dreams I've had about my patients.

She smiled. "It's funny you mentioned dreams. The nurses at Mayo have been having dreams about Monica ever since she arrived. In the dreams, they would talk to her as if she was perfectly healthy. They believe the dreams were a reminder to let them know that she can understand everything they were saying, in spite of how things look. The dreams are one reason why all the nurses took such an interest in her, and why they've treated her like a sister."

We arrived at the destination and transferred her to the bed. Her mother and I took turns giving report, but it didn't take long. The nurses were familiar with Monica. She'd been admitted there for eight days previously, but she became unstable and had to return to Mayo. They'd also fallen in love with her, and anxiously waited for her return. As the nurses fawned over their newest patient and long-lost friend, I washed my hands and quietly left the room. I love the way God orchestrates His plans—bringing strangers together to provide hope and healing through something as simple as dreams.

This transport gave me hope for our healthcare system. It was refreshing to meet people who sincerely cared about their patient and all of her needs.

cto

A few months later, I received this report from Monica's mother:

Hi!

Just wanted to give you a little update. She is now in an outpatient day program, is volunteering at the humane society, and they are actually talking about her starting back at school in the fall! PLEASE feel free to use her story as an example of God's wonderful work as you continue to minister (both physically and spiritually) to others.

Thanks again.
Liz

What You Really Need Is Doctor Jesus

I PICKED UP MY DAUGHTER from school today. She's not as young as she once was. She's enrolled in school to be a dental assistant. I let her drive us home. On the way, we decided to stop for coffee.

One problem with road coffee is consistency. One store's java can have decent flavor while a store down the street, under the same name, might serve coffee that tastes like sewer water. When it comes to coffee, my daughter and I prefer Circle K. The quality of their coffee is the best of the convenience stores we've been to. We got our usual, and as we approached the counter, I noticed that one of the cashiers had her left arm in a sling.

"Hey, how would you like to be healed?" I asked.

"Sure!" She replied.

We waited until the line of customers had dwindled to nothing, then introduced ourselves and asked what happened. "I was riding my bicycle to work when a car turned in front of me. I had to make a sudden stop, so I hit the brakes and went flying over the handle bars. That's how I injured my arm."

"We see a lot of people healed at gas stations. Would you like us to pray for you?" She agreed to let us have a whack at it. My daughter and I prayed together. We each placed a hand on her arm and together, we commanded the pain to leave, then asked if she felt anything.

"Your hands are really warm," she said to me.

I realized I'd been holding my cup of coffee, which naturally made my hands warmer. "That's just the heat from the coffee. Let me try it again." This time I held my hands a few inches away from her arm.

While we were praying for her, suddenly her co-worker asked, "Hey, will you guys heal my wrists?"

I yelled out, "Yes!"

The first woman still felt nothing, except my warm hands. "Don't be discouraged. Some healing takes time. Just believe you are healed." We approached the second woman and asked what was wrong.

"I have carpal tunnel in both wrists. I'm getting Prednisone injections every three months, because I don't want to have surgery."

"I don't think you need surgery. What you really need is Doctor Jesus." I asked if she wanted to be healed. She looked me straight in the eyes and said, "Yes."

"Hold out your arms." She held them out in front of me, and I placed my hands near her wrists, but I didn't actually touch her. I kept my hands a few inches away, so she wouldn't feel the warmth of my hands "Carpal tunnels, I command you to be open. Spirit of pain and inflammation, I command you to leave." I asked what she felt.

"Wow," she said, rubbing her wrists. "It feels warm in this one and the other one is tingling."

"That's the power of God healing you."

I asked her to put her arms out again and prayed a second time. Smiling, she said, "It's like I can feel the energy going into my wrists. Yeah... there's definitely an energy that I can feel."

We spoke with them for a few minutes about believing that they were healed. We told them God loved them, which they knew, since it seemed like they were both Christians. It's funny how the simple things like getting coffee at a convenience store can become God moments, if you're willing to take a chance.

Playing Chicken

BERNADETTE SAT IN A WHEELCHAIR as we rolled the gurney through the front door of her house. I glanced at her, then at her mother, and wondered who the patient was. "Hi," I said, as I reached my hand toward her mom. I introduced myself and my partner and asked her name. She told me hers and mentioned that she was partially blind and had difficulty hearing. I asked what brought us to her house today. Getting information from her was difficult, but she said we would be transporting her daughter.

Bernadette's life had been filled with medical setbacks ever since she was a young girl. At the age of 11, she suffered a severe diabetic seizure that left her with bilateral foot drop and other neurological problems. Recently, her gall bladder had been removed. They called us because she had been having chest pain since the procedure. She'd been evaluated at one of the emergency departments, but they found nothing and sent her home. We were going to take her to a different hospital for a second opinion, and to see her surgeon. Her countenance was sadder than a woman of twenty-something should have been. A deep sense of discomfort began stirring inside me.

Why was she so terribly sad?

We loaded her and got a set of vitals. I asked about starting an IV. "Don't bother. I have a port. You wouldn't be able to get an IV anyways. My veins are terrible."

I could see a small bulge in her skin in her right upper chest at the edge of her tank top strap, where the port was located. "OK... no IV," I said. We did an EKG, checked her blood sugar, and as we rolled down the road toward the hospital, I began asking questions. After getting the routine questions out of the way, I thought about asking if I could pray with her. I hesitated because for some reason, she seemed like the last person on earth who would want prayer. I couldn't put my finger on exactly why I thought she would say no. It just seemed like she wouldn't be interested.

One of the greatest problems I struggle with is the temptation to take the position that I have no responsibility to pray with my patients and nothing to lose if I decide not to ask if they want prayer. I wish I could say that I ask everyone I transport, but I don't.

"I have one more question to ask you Bernadette... would you like me to pray with you?"

Her face lit up with joy. "I know God heals people and I'd love to have you pray with me."

It was not the reaction I was expecting. She grabbed my hands in hers, closed her eyes and started thanking God. I asked the Holy Spirit to touch her and commanded pain to leave. We prayed and prayed and prayed. Then we talked. It turns out, Bernadette is a believer. Her husband is part of a group of men who go down to Mill Avenue in Tempe on Friday nights to pray with anyone who wants prayer. We had a lot to talk about.

We discussed her medical problems and the frustration her husband experienced because she hasn't been healed yet. I told her I have the same problem. I shared the strange fact that many people, who see the sick healed regularly, can't get their own family members healed. It seems that when I pray for my wife, my prayers bounce off the ceiling and fall helplessly to the floor.

Despite the fact that she hasn't been healed yet, Bernadette showed an amazing love for God. Her trust in Him was deeper than her outward appearance showed. My judgment of her willingness to have me pray with her wasn't even close to the truth. She loves Jesus, and she loves to pray, and she felt absolutely nothing in her body as I prayed with her. But the joy in her heart couldn't be hidden behind the Great Wall of China.

As we pulled in the driveway of the hospital, she began to perspire. "You better check my blood sugar again. When it starts to drop, it goes down fast." We did another check of her blood sugar. It was 60. We usually give a patient sugar if it's less than 70. We transferred her to the Emergency Department, I gave a quick report to the triage nurse then I got her a container of orange juice to drink. The nurse scowled at me. "What the heck are you doing?" she asked crossly.

"My patient's blood sugar is dropping."

"Well, she'll need more than one. I'll get another one. You take her to her room." We wheeled her to her room and moved her to the bed. I handed her the container of orange juice and told her not to be a stranger. She promised to keep in touch.

The Praying Nurse

WE PICKED UP OUR PATIENT at a nursing home. Susan was a few days post-operative for abdominal surgery. After spending less than 24 hours at the nursing home, she developed an abscess to her abdominal wall and needed to go back to the hospital.

As we drove, I told Susan I love to pray with my patients and asked if I could pray with her. She said yes, so I laid my hand on her shoulder and commanded inflammation, pain, and evil spirits to flee. She was grateful that I asked. We took her to her room and helped her transfer to the bed.

Then I went looking for her nurse. It didn't take long. She actually found me. I gave her my summary of the transport, "Nothing happened on the way here."

She replied, "Great! Where do I sign?" I handed her my clipboard and pointed to the signature box at the bottom. Another nurse came to the desk and made a comment about her hip hurting.

"Do you want to be healed?" I asked.

"I would love to be healed," she replied.

Looking at her ID badge, I saw that her name was Jayne.

"So Jayne, do you mind if I pray for you?"

"Sure, that would be fine."

She came over and stood next to me, closed her eyes and put her hand out. If I didn't know better, I'd swear she'd been following me around. She knew too much. Who puts their hands out when you pray for them? "Jayne, how bad is the pain on a one-to-ten scale?"

"It hurts pretty bad."

"Okay. You're a nurse right? So on a scale from one to ten, how bad is your pain?"

"Oh, I'm sorry. It's about an eight."

Her hand was still outstretched as if she was expecting me to hold it. I asked if I could put my hand on her hip, which she agreed to. "Holy Spirit, bring your presence." I immediately felt His glory arrive. "Spirit of pain, I command you to leave in the name of Jesus. Inflammation, get out now. Bones and connective tissue, be healed. What do you feel, Jayne?"

She moved her hips around. "Wow, it doesn't hurt anymore! How would you like to pray for my lower back?"

"Well, I would be delighted to," I replied as I put my hand on her back. "Pain and inflammation, leave now in the name of Jesus. Bones and discs, be healed." I asked what she felt. She bent sideways to test out her back.

"That's amazing. All the pain is gone! Do you have time to do my neck?" I placed my hand on her neck and repeated the process.

While praying for her neck, I closed my eyes and saw a vision of her raising her arms. When the Holy Spirit shows you something like this in a vision, it's a good idea to have the person do exactly what you see. "Hey Jayne, would you do me a favor and raise both of your arms?" I still had my eyes closed as I commanded pain to leave. When I opened my eyes I saw another nurse standing next to Jayne with one hand on her shoulder. She was praying with me. I was stunned. I'd never had a nurse or doctor join me when praying for someone in a hospital, so I thanked her for joining us. She just stood there smiling as she prayed.

I asked Jayne to check out her neck. She moved her head around and said the pain was gone. I looked around and realized the other nurse had disappeared.

I spent a few minutes teaching Jayne how to keep her healing. "I'm glad you've been healed, but you should know there's a chance the pain might return. Healing is warfare. There's a kingdom of darkness that wants us to suffer, and there is God's kingdom. God wants us to be healed. I work for Him and I can get you healed, but it's up to you to keep your healing. If the pain returns, you can do the same thing I did. Just command the pain to leave in the name of Jesus."

Ninety Minutes with Mary

"HELP ME, DOCTOR. I DON'T feel good." I leaned closer to my patient who was strapped to the gurney and softly said, "I know you don't feel good, Mary. That's why we're taking you to the hospital."

"Doctor... I'm in a lot of pain. You gotta help me."

"I'm sorry Mary. I know you're in pain."

"You don't know, doctor. You have no idea how bad it hurts."

We arrived at the emergency department and took our place in line behind another crew at the registration desk. As we waited in the hallway for a bed, Mary struggled to get off the gurney. In her weakened condition it was easy for me to keep her on the gurney with one hand. She quickly grew tired and gave up.

I've been haunted by memories of Mary for a month now. Images of her thin, emaciated body seem to be forever etched in my mind. It's easy to forget most patients if you try. But not Mary. We picked her up at a mental health unit where she'd been vomiting coffee-ground emesis for two days. Her hospital gown seemed to wrap around her gaunt frame forever. I can't recall transporting anyone who looked so malnourished. It wasn't just her size. It was everything.

Her eyes were dull and lifeless and she couldn't seem to focus them on anything. When she spoke, her mouth barely moved. Her tongue was dry and cracked. Her lips were a sickly, blue color. Her matted hair looked like it hadn't been washed in months. Her fingers were bony with raw, cracked skin on her knuckles.

Thinking that I was her husband, Mary spoke again. "I need to go home, honey."

"Mary, please lie on the bed and wait. They'll have a room for you soon."

"When? It's been so long, honey. I can't wait any more."

"They'll have a bed soon."

"Honey, you gotta take me home, now. I don't feel good."

"Mary, please be patient."

"I hurt honey, real bad. My back hurts so bad. I need a pain pill."

"Mary, I'll ask the nurse to get you something for pain when they get you a bed."

The nurse's station was busy. It was shift change. I overheard one nurse tell her replacement that they'd been slammed with ambulances in the last hour and had no beds left. When an uninvited guest comes to a party and there are no chairs left, one solution is to ignore them until someone leaves. We were the uninvited guest.

Mary's restlessness couldn't be soothed. Every few minutes she tried to get off the gurney or begged us to take her home. She was terribly confused, having no clue who we were or where she was. After a patient left the emergency department, the crew in front of us descended on the now vacant bed and unloaded their patient.

"Doctor… I need a pain pill. I hurt real bad."

"I know you hurt Mary, and I'm sorry."

"You don't know doctor. You don't understand. I need a pain pill."

Closing my eyes, I laid my head on the rail of the gurney and prayed silently, commanding pain to leave. I felt absolutely useless, trapped in what seemed like a hopeless situation. "Holy Spirit, bring your peace upon her."

"You don't know, doctor. You don't know how bad I hurt. I can't stay here. I need to go home." She tried to get off the gurney again, but I held her in place. Minutes seemed like hours.

A nurse came over and asked what her story was. I gave him what information I had. He asked if she had an IV. I told him no. She was so dehydrated, that her veins were completely collapsed. My IV attempts failed. He brought an IV tray over to the gurney and tried to find a vein to draw blood from, but he had no luck. He was as frustrated as I was. We had already been in the hallway for an hour. He didn't like leaving us there, but there was nowhere else to put her. He had other things to take care of so he left. I had nothing else to do but wait. A few minutes later, another crew arrived with a patient. It was the same crew that was waiting for a bed when we arrived.

"I need to go home, honey. I can't stay here."

"Mary, you're very sick. You need to stay in the hospital."

"No, honey, take me home. I can't stay here. My back hurts so bad."

"I know you hurt, Mary. The nurse will give you something for pain when we get you in a bed."

"You don't know. You don't know how bad it is. I need a pain pill, honey."

Mary's cycle of confusion and my time of testing continued for another half hour until a room finally opened up. Ninety minutes after we arrived, we moved her to the bed and I gave report to the nurse.

I've heard of long ER waits in urban hospitals. Legend has it the wait can be as long as two or three hours in crowded, urban hospitals. I can't imagine working in a system like that. I also can't imagine how Mary came to be in this condition living at a mental health hospital.

In just 90 minutes, Mary had the opportunity to test just about every aspect of my character: Patience, politeness, professionalism, compassion, and my willingness to pray. I'm certain that God gave me a truck load of compassion that day. There's no other way to explain how I managed to avoid losing my composure. I'll probably never forget Mary, though at times, I wish I could.

In eternity, I'll relive this event one more time. And I'll get a chance to see things through Mary's dull, unfocused eyes. In that day, everything will be clear and sharp. Every thought exposed. Every detail revealed. The motives and intentions of my heart laid bare. I can't help but wonder what that will be like.

My Brother's Keeper

SURROUNDED BY STRANGERS SEEKING RELIEF from their aches and pains, Patty sat beside me in a wheelchair in the Emergency Department waiting room. We picked her up at a clinic, where she was evaluated for a possible head injury. She struck her head on a door and had blurred vision and a headache. We talked in the ambulance on the way to the hospital and she shared the following story:

"I had great plans for my future when I was young. I'd always dreamed of working as a police officer, so I attended a law enforcement academy after I graduated High School. During my first job interview, they asked about my health. I was honest and told them I have a condition that makes me a little forgetful and disoriented sometimes. They turned me down and advised me to consider another career. I interviewed with the department of corrections, for a job as a prison guard, but they turned me down for the same reason. It seemed I wasn't going to get a job in law enforcement, so I decided to take a job at a bank. I did pretty well and eventually I was promoted to a management position until the banking crisis in 2008. I lost my job and so did a lot of other people. As I got older, I developed more medical problems. My friends said I should apply for government assistance because of my disability, but I hated the idea of taking money without working for it."

We arrived at the Emergency Department. Patty didn't have a serious condition and the ED was crowded so we were directed to the waiting room, which meant it could be several hours before she would be seen by a doctor. She didn't complain. I helped her to a wheelchair and took a seat beside her and waited to give my report to the triage nurse.

As I waited, I began to feel an overwhelming sense of compassion for her. I wanted to end the string of disappointments and give her one small victory to restore her hope in God.

"Patty, how would you like to be healed?" I was stepping out on a limb, since I didn't know exactly what she needed to be healed of yet. The description of her medical problems was vague. But God knew what she needed, and I figured He'd take care of the details.

"I'd love to be healed," she replied, as her eyes filled up with tears.

My eyes misted over as I placed my hand on her shoulder. "Holy Spirit, bring your presence near and touch this dear woman." I felt His presence immediately. "Sickness and disease, leave now in the name of Jesus." I asked if she felt anything.

"My legs are tingling."

"What's wrong with your legs?"

"I have a lot of trouble with them."

"Well you don't anymore, because God is healing them. Would you like Him to heal your mind?"

"I would."

I placed my hand on the back of her head. "Memories, be healed. Evil spirits, I command you to leave. Brain, I command you to be free of all neurological conditions." I asked what she felt.

Moving her hands to feel her face, she said, "Wow... my whole head is tingling."

We sat in the waiting room crying like a couple of babies, as God gave her a complete makeover from head to toe. I taught her how to keep her healing. All of this must have looked strange to the triage nurse, who came over and said, "I'm ready to see her."

I wheeled her to the exam room and gave the nurse my report. Patty thanked me then gave me a hug and I left to find a place where I could finish my paperwork. When I was done with my report, I returned to the triage desk and gave them a copy. The nurse who took it asked if I would write down my contact information for Patty. She told them she'd been healed. The nurse wanted my contact information too. She was a Christian and wanted to know more about healing, so I told her how to find my website.

I came to the realization that God often draws us into encounters like this one through our feelings. The compassion I felt while sitting next to Patty didn't come from me. It came from God. Our spirit has the ability to sense different emotions like joy, sorrow or compassion.

In this encounter God allowed me to feel His compassion for Patty as if it were my own so that I would be moved to intervene on His behalf. We often wait on God to do something to help others, but many times He is waiting on us to sense how He feels toward them and release what He wants to do. I wonder how often I've felt God's heart for someone, only to reason away those feelings, because it's easier to believe that their fate isn't my responsibility. Part of the responsibility of being an ambassador of heaven is acknowledging that I am my brother's keeper.

Not Very Religious

I'VE BEEN SPENDING A LOT of time lately inside gas stations. If I'm not buying coffee, I'm buying water. Summer is here and the weather is sizzling hot, and God is healing people wherever we go. As I approached the checkout stand, I saw a woman wearing an immobilizer on her leg. She had a noticeable limp. I made a simple comment as she passed. "Wow, that looks like it hurts."

"It hurts all the time," she replied.

"Do you mind telling me how it happened?"

"I broke it, but when I went to my doctor, he said it was just a sprain. I went through physical therapy and it wasn't getting any better, so I got a second opinion. Turns out I had two broken bones, and they put a cast on my foot. The cast didn't help and the doctor decided to try this immobilizer. I've been wearing it for eight months, but it still isn't any better."

We paid for our things and I asked if she had a few minutes to talk. We walked outside and sat on a stone wall in front of the building. I thought I might as well get right to the point. "Would you have any desire to be healed by God?"

With a smirk, she said, "I need to tell you something."

For the next ten minutes she recalled different events from her childhood. I thought she would eventually tell me why she didn't believe in God. Then she shared a recent story about being bitten by a venomous snake. "When the ambulance arrived, they didn't know how to treat the snake bite, so they pulled out a first aid manual and began reading it in my living room, hoping to find instructions on what to do. I was getting weaker and they needed to get me to a hospital soon. I told them to call for a helicopter to fly me to a hospital before I died. The helicopter landed six miles from my house so they put me in the ambulance and drove me to the landing zone. I remember like it was yesterday... as the helicopter lifted off into the sky, my body and spirit separated and I found myself standing before God in eternity. It was the most awesome experience I ever had."

I told her about my love of near-death stories. She told me about meeting her parents again and what is felt like to be surrounded by the all-consuming love of the Father. We talked about the absolute sense of peace in eternity. After she finished her story, I asked if I could pray for her foot to be healed.

With a bit of apprehension, she said, "I'm not one of those people who goes to church every week. I believe in God, but I'm not very religious."

"I don't go to church either. I work every Sunday. I see Jesus a little differently than most people. He's the kind of guy who met strangers wherever He found them and wasn't afraid to be friends with the sinners that religious people looked down on."

She smiled in agreement. "You can pray for my foot now, if you want."

I placed my hand on her ankle. "Holy Spirit, I ask you to touch this young lady. Ligaments, nerves, tendons, bones, and cartilage, be healed in the name of Jesus." I asked what she felt.

She pointed to her toes. "It's tingling right there."

"God's beginning to heal your foot." Her smile grew bigger.

I placed my hand on the immobilizer again and commanded more healing and asked what she felt.

"Now my ankle is tingling."

"Pain, inflammation and swelling, I command you to leave. Ligaments, muscles, tendons and bones, be healed." I asked a third time what she felt.

"Now the back of my leg is tingling, just below my calf muscle."

"Is there any pain at all?"

She flexed her foot. "No. It's gone."

"Are you lying?" I asked as I began to laugh.

Laughing with me, she said, "I'm not lying, it doesn't hurt at all. It's completely gone."

We sat in the shade and sipped our drinks. I told her that God loves her. I taught her how to keep her healing and explained what to do if the pain returned. She thanked me for taking time to pray with her.

Her Best Shift Ever

MY REGULAR PARTNER CALLED OUT sick, so Kari was my partner for the next eight hours. We were having a very slow day, which gave us time to talk. She told me about her life. She was interested in archaeology and earned a Master's degree, then began working on her PhD. Near the end of the process she ran out of money and never completed her doctorate. As a temporary way to earn a paycheck, she went to EMT school. After discussing her own life for a while, she asked about mine. What plans did a guy my age have for the future?

I told her that I'd worked in nearly every type of EMS environment, and that I'd went through every career stage you can go through, from an excited newbie to an experienced trainer to a burned-out, jaded veteran. Then I told her about the dreams that began in 2008. Hundreds of dreams about praying for people in the ambulance. I shared a few healing testimonies with her. She was a little shocked, but she wanted to know more about what God was doing in my life, so I shared a few more stories. She asked if I could help with a few of her medical problems. "I thought you'd never ask," I replied.

She asked if I'd pray for her father to be healed of chronic back pain then related the tragic tale of her best friend, who was severely injured in a car accident. She had a metal plate in her foot that was slowly separating from the bone it was screwed to. It caused severe pain and her surgeon didn't think anything could be done about it. "I'd be happy to pray for both of them," I said.

"I've worn glasses for years because I'm near-sighted. I'd love it if my eyes could be healed and I didn't need to wear these glasses anymore."

"No point in wasting time. Let's get to work." I placed my hand on her forehead just above her eyes. "I command these eyes to be healed in the name of Jesus." I asked if she felt anything.

"Yeah, I do." Feeling her lower eyelids, she said, "It feels warm right here, under my eyes." She removed her glasses and noticed that her distant vision was improving. She was surprised at how quickly her vision changed.

I placed my hand on her forehead again. "Holy Spirit, bring more of your healing power. Corneas, retinas and all parts of the eye, be healed. Check your vision again."

She removed her glasses and looked around. "It's not perfect yet, but it's better."

I placed my hand on her forehead one more time. "Spirit of blindness, come out. Eyes, be healed in Jesus' name." I had her check her vision one more time.

She looked at a sign about 100 feet in the distance. "That's amazing. I can read that sign over there. There's no way I could read it before without my glasses."

Satisfied with the improvement, she asked if I'd pray for her neck and shoulders to be healed. Like most of us who work in EMS, she suffers from chronic muscle strain and fatigue. She felt as if her neck and upper back muscles were under constant tension, causing a nagging pain that would not go away.

I placed my hand near the back of her neck, just above her shirt collar, but I didn't actually touch her. As I commanded her muscles to be healed, I felt something I've never felt before. Heat.

I felt waves of heat coming from her upper back, just below my hand. She felt it too. "Let me see your hand," she said.

I held my hand out in front of her. She felt my palm. "That's crazy. When you put your hand near my neck, I felt heat coming from it, almost like a hot pack. But your palm feels normal."

"I know. It is kinda crazy. I feel it too." She moved her shoulders around. All the pain was gone.

We talked some more, because she had a lot of questions, which I answered the best I could. She understood that I'm something like a conduit for God's power, which flows through me and heals people. I told her, "The only reason God's power flows through me, is because Jesus gave me the authority to heal people just as He gave the same authority to all of His disciples."

She looked at me and said, "This has probably been the best shift of my career."

I Once Was Lost

WE TRANSPORTED A PATIENT FROM a nursing home to a hospital for an abdominal CT scan. This was the second day in a row that we transported him for the same procedure. The previous day, we brought him to radiology only to learn that his insurance company had not yet authorized the test. So we took him back after waiting for an hour. Today, the insurance approval went through. While waiting in line for an open scanner room, a nurse came by and asked if we'd been helped. I told her we had, and then I noticed an immobilizer on her wrist and asked if she wanted to be healed.

With a puzzled look on her face, she asked what I meant. "I pray with people and God heals them," I replied. She seemed to understand, but I could tell she was nervous about praying in a busy hospital corridor. I took her aside to an alcove out of the main flow of traffic. "If you want to be healed, it will only take a minute." She agreed to let me pray with her. I asked the Holy Spirit to bring His presence and immediately I felt lightness and joy come over me. (I'd be lying if I said I didn't enjoy this part of the job.)

I commanded ligaments, tendons, bones, nerves and muscles to be healed then asked, "What do you feel?"

"Tingling... and it feels better."

I repeated the process and asked again how she felt.

She smiled. "The pain is completely gone!"

I asked if she was serious. She was. Her wrist was completely healed. I told her that's how God is. He heals us because He loves us. She had to go back to work but it was obvious she was tickled to be healed.

The next transport was to a nursing home. After dropping off our patient, I gave report to the nurse. My partner took the gurney outside to clean it. After giving report, I stepped into a hallway and realized I was lost. I walked to the end of the hallway and checked in both directions, looking for something familiar. I found another hallway that I didn't recognize, and there were no obvious clues pointing to the way out. I decided to go back to the nurse's station at the other end of the hallway, but I didn't want look like an idiot.

How do you ask for directions to the front door and not look foolish?

I found a nurse who didn't seem too busy and asked if she'd point me in the direction of the front door. She politely gave me the route and I asked how she injured her wrist. She looked at the immobilizer on her wrist and said, "I don't know. I've had a CAT scan, an MRI, and all kinds of tests and they can't determine what's wrong with it. It's swollen and it hurts like crazy.

"Would you like to be healed?"

"I'd love that," she said with a grin. "I was at a healing meeting last night. I do Reiki healing." I wondered to myself why she wasn't healed at the Reiki meeting. I thought about asking her, but I kept it to myself.

"Do you want to be healed?"

"Yes."

"Are you certain?"

"Absolutely."

I asked the Holy Spirit to bring His presence. A few seconds later, my cares melted away as I stood in His glory, commanding her wrist to be healed in the mighty name of Jesus. We were a little intoxicated with joy when another nurse came by and looked at us strangely. "We're just having a special moment here," she said with a giggle. I laughed inside and thought, it's just as special for me as it is for you. I asked how she felt. She looked at her wrist and moved it around. "It feels good."

"Take off the brace, I guarantee you it's healed."

Releasing the Velcro straps, she pulled off the brace and tested her range of motion. "Wow... that's amazing. It doesn't hurt. There's still a bit of swelling, but it doesn't hurt at all."

"That's how God is, my friend. He doesn't do anything half way. The swelling will go down in a little while; you'll see. You might consider getting rid of the wrist brace and not putting it back on. I believe you're healed for good and if the pain comes back, instead of putting the brace back on, just tell the pain to leave in the name of Jesus."

Doomsday Preppers

---∞∞∞---

WHEN SOME PEOPLE THINK ABOUT survivalists, or as they're affectionately called, "doomsday preppers" they think of gun-toting weirdos with an affinity for gas masks and gold. I recently met a couple of preppers and they aren't the kind of people I thought they would be.

I had a dream one night about meeting up with survivalists in my area and joining their group. My wife and I decided to check out the local "prepper" groups to see if we could find someone to talk to. We located a guy who was interested in sharing information on prepping. We exchanged e-mails and had a long phone conversation that ended with an invitation for us to visit him. We took him up on the offer the next day.

We drove to his house, which is located in a very nice neighborhood. I didn't see any machine gun turrets or signs of a bomb shelter—just a nice woodworking shop that made me a bit envious. Frank showed us around and proudly described the unique features of the home he built by himself. It was a beautiful day so we sat on the back porch where we chatted for the next eight hours about all things related to prepping.

Before moving to Arizona, I lived in Washington for 16 years where we suffered frequent power outages. Eventually, I decided to buy a generator so I could make coffee for myself and the neighbors during the frequent windstorms there. I've always liked the outdoors. I've been a rock-climber since I was a kid. As an adult I took up mountaineering and eventually became interested in high-angle rescue. As a firefighter, I was trained to teach community preparedness for disasters like earthquakes and tsunamis. During the last few years, I've been having concerning dreams about future events, so I began setting aside more emergency supplies.

I've slowly been developing the lifestyle of a prepper. I may not be an expert in preparedness, but I know a little about it, and I'm learning more as time goes on. I knew from the phone conversation we had earlier that Frank was an expert on prepping, though he cringed every time I mentioned the word "expert." We came to his house to learn and my wife, ever the good student, brought a notebook full of questions she'd written out beforehand.

Preppers and prophetic people have a lot in common. They both have an eye on the future. The Old Testament is full of people who could have been called preppers. Noah spent 120 years building an ark for a flood, although it had never rained before. Joseph is the prototype of what modern preppers are all about. Pharaoh had a dream about disaster and Joseph interpreted it. He saw famine and drought coming. He told Pharaoh what he saw coming and developed a plan to mitigate the damage. He instructed Pharaoh to set aside a little each year, to get the nation though the time of hardship. It worked perfectly and a nation was saved, all because of a prepper.

I had an ulterior motive when I met with Frank and his wife. I explained to him on the phone that I thought preppers were missing out on one major thing that could make their work of preparing for disaster a lot easier.

They seldom consider the miraculous.

Medical care in a disaster is a huge concern for preppers. Their theory is that medical care may not be available in a worst-case scenario, so it's wise to have someone on your team who can treat illness and injuries. Most preppers recruit doctors, nurses, or ideally, combat medics for their team so that in a disaster, they have someone around with experience in medicine. I suggested to Frank that there's a better solution.

Preppers hold the view that one day there will be a lack of the things needed to survive. They believe that the best strategy is to store up what will be needed, because no one will provide it for them. My view is that there may be lack in the kingdoms of man, but there is never a lack in the kingdom of God, and that my Father is *willing* and *able* to meet all my needs through His riches.

I told Frank, "Someone who is trained in divine healing would be indispensable in a crisis, since it doesn't require a license to practice and you don't need any equipment or drugs. Divine healing has no side-effects and it can be done over distances. Better yet, it can be done by anyone who is a disciple of Jesus, if they know how to release the power of the kingdom. If you have someone who can heal the sick and injured, you don't need to stockpile medical supplies or worry about having a doctor on your team."

I went one step further. "Some of my friends have prayed over empty gas tanks and then drove their cars hundreds of miles to church meetings without filling up their tank. I have friends who have taken a few dozen hot dogs and buns to feed the poor and when hundreds of people show up, they prayed over the food and it fed everyone with some left over."

He understood my perspective, but for most people, seeing is believing. I wanted to demonstrate the reality of the kingdom to him, so he could see it firsthand. I knew from our phone conversation that Frank suffered from Crohn's disease, but what I didn't know was that his wife had a torn meniscus in her right knee.

When I pray with a group of people who have various medical problems, I try to select someone to heal first whose healing can be verified immediately, without medical testing. One healing miracle at the beginning encourages everyone else who needs healing. The best candidates to start with are people with orthopedic injuries like sprains, fractures, torn ligaments, torn cartilage, etc. Chronic back pain is a common complaint for many people. These injuries are usually painful and they limit range of motion. When healing manifests, the pain disappears and range of motion returns. The miracle can be verified immediately, without medical testing.

I wanted Frank to be healed, but I thought that if he saw his wife healed first, it would encourage him. So I asked if she wanted to be healed.

She said, "I would love to be healed."

She was sitting in a chair, so I placed my hand on her knee. "Spirit of pain, get out now. Inflammation, leave. Meniscus, I command you to be healed in the name of Jesus." I had her stand up. What happened next was a shocker to me. I could see that she was standing slightly tilted to one side. With a stunned look on her face she asked, "Why can't I stand up straight? It feels like one of my legs is too long!" She took off the shoe on her right foot and removed a heel lift she had inside it. She put her shoe back on and said, "Oh my God, I think my short leg just got longer. I don't need my heel lift anymore!"

To test her knee, she got down on the floor and sat on her legs with both knees bent. She leaned as hard as she could on the right knee but couldn't make the pain return. She was healed and pretty darn happy about it. Frank looked at her in disbelief.

He went in the house to make some chili dogs for us and then returned to the porch. We talked and shared stories and enjoyed the evening with our new friends. We really like these folks. But it was time for Frank to be healed, so I got up and stood behind him. "Frank, it looks like it's time for you to meet your maker." He cringed and shook his head as I placed my hand on his abdomen. "Sickness and inflammation, leave now. Lord, I bless the work of healing you're about to do." I sat down and asked what he felt.

"This is really weird. We just ate, right? Now right as you were praying, I became very hungry again."

"I think the hunger is a sign that you're healed." We talked a bit more about healing and God. When it was nearly midnight, we made our way to our car and bid them farewell.

౭౦

A few days later, I received an e-mail from Frank. Here's part of the report he gave me:

"... On a side note, (my wife's) knee still feels good, and I have not had any symptoms to the magnitude that is normal. Go figure??? Not a complete believer yet, but am keeping the door open!"

I kept in touch with Frank, and a year after we first met, he had no signs of the Crohn's disease that he suffered with since he was a teenager.

Miracle at the Wound Care Clinic

ONE OF THE MAJOR PROBLEMS with patients who are confined to a bed is that they tend to develop decubitus ulcers, more commonly known as "bed sores." Just a short time spent in the same position, puts pressure on tissues of the body. The pressure reduces blood flow. Reduced blood flow impedes the exchange of oxygen, nutrients, and removal of waste products. This process can result in the death of body tissue. The death of tissue leads to open sores in the skin, which become infected and painful. People who can't change body positions on their own are susceptible to these skin ulcers. Many patients have them.

Today, we transported one such patient to clinic for wound care. The wound care office was busy. Workers hurried from room to room, moving patients around, but one woman named Kate, wasn't moving so fast. An immobilizer on her leg made her walk a little slower than everyone else.

Our patient wouldn't be seen immediately, so we parked our gurney in the hall, and as Kate passed by, I asked why she wore the immobilizer. She seemed glad to have a reason to take a break and filled me in on the details. Several weeks earlier, she stepped off a curb and tore the supporting structures in her ankle including her Achilles tendon which detached from the heel.

"Have you had surgery yet?"

"Not yet. My doctor wanted me to try an immobilizer for a few weeks before doing surgery."

"How would you like to be healed?"

She looked at me suspiciously. "Exactly what do you have in mind?" I told her about a few people that had been healed recently. "Sounds great. I'll give it a shot."

"Tell you what," I said. "When the doctor is seeing my patient, I'll catch up with you and we can get you healed."

When the time arrived, we rolled our patient into an exam room, gave a quick report, and let them to do their thing. That gave me 20 minutes to get Kate's foot healed. I went to the receptionist desk where Kate worked and told her I was ready. We walked to the staff break room to avoid drawing attention. Sometimes a crowd is appropriate for miracles, but in the workplace, I try to respect people's need for privacy.

We sat down and I explained what I usually do. I asked about her level of pain and range of motion, and then I shared a few testimonies, including the people who had recently been healed of a torn Achilles tendon. I placed my hand on the immobilizer near her ankle. "You're probably going to feel either heat or tingling. Spirits of pain and inflammation, I command you to leave. Holy Spirit, bring your presence. Ligaments, tendons, bones, nerves and blood vessels, be healed." I asked what she felt.

"You know it's funny you mentioned tingling. As soon as you started speaking I felt tingling on the side of my foot by your hand."

"Achilles tendon, I command you to reattach to the heel right now, in the name of Jesus. What do you feel now?"

"Now the tingling is up in my calf, which is where the tendon is torn."
Is there any pain at all?"

She moved her foot around. "Nope. It's all gone."

"I'm pretty sure that your foot is completely healed. If you'd like, you can probably take the immobilizer off."

"I think you're right. It does seem to be healed. I don't think I need this thing anymore, but I think I'll leave it on until I get home."

We had a little more time before I had to get back to my patient, so I gave her a quick lesson on how to keep her healing. "Healing is a battle. God wants you to be healed, but the enemy wants you to live in pain. Sometimes you need to push back against the enemy. You saw what I did to get you healed, so if the pain comes back, command it to leave in the name of Jesus, like I did. Then continue to believe you're healed."

Wayne's Story

WAYNE SAT IN A CHAIR waiting as residents and staff at the mental health hospital whizzed past. Wearing a red baseball cap and a smile, he made his way to the gurney and we fastened the seat belts. His skin was red—almost as rosy as his hat. "How are you feeling, Wayne?" I asked.

"Pretty weak. And I think I'm dehydrated."

He struck me as the kind of guy you could ask just about anything and he'd give you a straight answer. I did the introductions as we raised the gurney to load height. The door opened and a blur of residents swarmed past. Most of them said hi to Wayne. Some asked where he was going. "I'm not feeling well so they're taking me to the hospital." It was obvious he was well-liked.

We were notified by dispatch before going on scene that Wayne has HIV. My mind went where it always goes when we transport a patient with HIV. I'd love to tell you that I don't wonder about a patient's sexual past when I hear that they have HIV. But I wonder about a lot of things, like whether they know Jesus or not. I try to keep an open mind. I've been wrong so many times before. As we headed toward the elevator, Wayne told his friends he was disappointed to be going to the hospital. He was looking forward to leading the Bible study tonight.

We rolled Wayne toward the ambulance and talked on the way. He'd been vomiting and having diarrhea for three days and hadn't slept in two. Considering how sick he was, he had a great attitude... and great big veins.

I got the IV supplies ready and told him about the first time I transported a patient with HIV. It was out of a hospital in Nashville, in

1988. HIV was a new disease. We did mouth-to-mouth on dead people who would usually vomit in our mouth, and we *never* wore gloves. The man we transported that day was brutally beaten because he was gay. He was a bloody mess from head to toe and we were transferring him to another hospital because he didn't have insurance. They didn't tell us he had HIV until we were almost out the door. They were afraid that if they did, we'd refuse to take him. Times have changed since then—mostly for the better.

The IV went in easily. As the fluids began to rehydrate his parched body, my partner disappeared behind the closing rear door of the ambulance. Wayne and I talked all the way to the hospital, mostly about eternity. I told him I collected stories about people who had died and gone to heaven then returned. He asked what I thought about the teaching that people "sleep" when they die. I replied, "I think the idea of soul sleep is a lot of nonsense. It's my belief that when our physical body dies, we go immediately into the presence of God. To be absent from the body is to be present with the Lord."

I shared some of the testimonies I'd heard from people who had died, including a man we'd transported earlier in the day. He'd been run over by a Humvee and went into cardiac arrest. In eternity he saw a line that he was standing on. He knew that if he went one way, he would be sent back to earth, and if he went the other way, he would stay in eternity. "Wayne, I'd like to pray for you to be healed."

"Man, I would love that," he replied.

I rested my hand on his shoulder. "I bless the work of God in Wayne's life. I command sickness to leave in the name of Jesus." The ambulance filled with the heavy presence of God's glory. Peace and joy took up residence in our little corner of the world.

We talked a little more and he told me a story from his childhood. "When I was about seven or eight years old I wandered around town for a couple of days. No one acknowledged I was there. It was like I'd become invisible. The second day I heard the Lord tell me when I was thirsty to put my mouth to the ground and open it and when I did, my thirst disappeared. I didn't need to drink any water. God made water come up from the ground to quench my thirst."

Wayne had known the Lord from childhood. We talked about heaven and about how people say that our existence there is a lot like being a child. There is no fear of anything—just a complete innocence and a knowing that your Father is perfect and all that He makes is perfect.

We talked about the perfect love He surrounds us with. In the short time we had together I developed a real love for Wayne, and I was honored to be able to pray for him.

ICU Healed

ONE DAY WE TRANSPORTED A patient who had Lou Gehrig's disease. He had been diagnosed years earlier, and was now completely paralyzed, except for his facial muscles. Because he was paralyzed, he was unable to breathe on his own, and he was dependent on a ventilator for every breath. This story is about the respiratory therapist who was on duty when we picked him up in the ICU. As we got our patient ready, I noticed the respiratory therapist rubbing her right shoulder as if it hurt.

"What's wrong with your shoulder?" I asked.

"I tore my rotator cuff last year when a nurse jerked a code cart away from me."

"Any chance you'd let me get you healed?"

"That would be great!"

I walked over to where she was standing and placed my hand gently on her shoulder. "I command pain and inflammation to leave in the name of Jesus. Ligaments, cartilage, muscle and bones, be healed." Standing at the nurse's station in front of everyone I asked if she felt anything.

"It just feels a little warm."

"Cool. That's the power of God healing you." I commanded her shoulder to be healed a second time. When I was done, I said, "I want you to try to raise your arm up as high as you can." She tried, but with her arm only slightly raised it hurt. "Okay, no worries. It might take a few minutes for the healing to completely manifest." We continued getting our patient ready. She left the room but returned a few minutes later. Raising her arm a little higher than before, she said, "Look what I can do, I haven't been able to do this in over a year!"

We needed help getting all our equipment down to the ambulance, so the respiratory therapist volunteered to escort us. On the way to the ambulance, she told the patient's wife I healed her shoulder. "Are you sure you're healed?" I asked.

"I know I am!" She raised her arm up even higher to prove it. We loaded the patient and our equipment, and I pulled out my phone to take a picture of her holding the patient's balloons with her arm raised up high. She had a huge smile on her face. You never know who God will touch next, so be open to any possibilities.

Prince of Peace

WE ARRIVED AT THE EMERGENCY Department to transport Alfred to another hospital. From his bed he sent another text message. His wife gave him a hug and his nurse gave me report. He came in because he'd been having chest pain for two days, but according to the nurse, he had been pain-free since he arrived. His cardiac enzymes were slightly elevated, so he was being transferred to a hospital with cardiology services. His chief complaint now was a killer headache. I introduced myself and I asked him a few questions.

"Are you having any chest pain now, Alfred?"

"No, just a real bad headache."

His wife interrupted. "Why don't you tell them about the chest pain?" His wife ratted him out. He sent her a text about an hour ago saying he was having chest pain. But he didn't tell the nurse. He was afraid. He wasn't sure what would happen if he told them he was having chest pain again. In his mind, he was too young for a heart attack. I glanced at his registration sheet and found the check box for religious preference. He was a non-denominational Christian. We got a set of vitals and got him loaded in the ambulance. After we were underway, I took a seat next to him.

"Hey Alfred, I have a question for you... would you like me to pray with you?"

"That would be great," he replied with a friendly smile. Alfred had been under a lot of stress lately, much more than he's used to and the chest pain only created more stress.

"On a scale from one to ten, how bad is your headache?"

"About an eight."

I placed my hand gently on his shoulder and asked the Holy Spirit to bring His presence and touch Alfred. "Spirit of pain, I command you to leave. Holy Spirit, touch him with your power and remove all sickness and pain from him. I bless your work of healing and Lord; I thank you for your mercy." I continued praying for a few minutes and asked what he felt.

"It's gone. It's all gone." He said, slightly amazed.

"Your headache?"

"Yeah."

"Are you lying to me?"

"No, I'm not lying. As soon as you put your hand on me and started praying, it left. It was like... two seconds later."

We both smiled and laughed and talked about how amazing God is. Not only was his headache gone, but so was all of his anxiety and fear. "I feel this amazing peace like I've never felt before."

"Dude, that's because Jesus, the Prince of Peace, is here." We talked the rest of the way about healing, the kingdom, and the goodness of God. I taught him about faith and healing and what to do if the symptoms returned. When we picked him up at the Emergency Department, he was a nervous wreck. When we dropped him off at the other hospital, he was smiling and laughing. His wife must have wondered what happened to him along the way.

Jesus happened to him.

The Banker – A Person of Peace

THE ECONOMIC COLLAPSE OF 2008 left many of us with some bitterness toward the banking industry. Bankers themselves have received of a lot of criticism since then. My trip to Australia put me in close contact with a very unusual banker. And what I've experienced since meeting him has changed my perspective on bankers.

The banker I would meet had created a successful life for himself, but his life wasn't always one of fortune. He spent his younger days in Europe and for a season, was unable to find work, finally hiring on as a manual laborer in London. He lived in a tiny house with a group of roughnecks. One night, he was jumped by thugs who robbed him, beat him up and tossed him in a rubbish bin. Were it not for a good-hearted stranger, who found him and called for an ambulance, things could have turned out even worse. Over time, he married a wonderful and gifted woman, secured a good paying job, and became the proud father of two charming children. One day, he had a long talk with his wife. He asked her, "Do you want to have an ordinary life or an extraordinary life?"

His wife responded, "Well obviously, I want an extraordinary life."

They then spoke about what they should do with their lives and resources. It didn't take long to agree that the best thing they could do with the abundance God had provided was to become generous givers. They saw money not as something to be treasured, but as a tool to be used to bless others.

The banker had been raised as a Christian by his Pentecostal mother, though he'd never been a very spiritual person. One day, while building

95

a wall on his property, he heard the clear and distinct voice of God tell him it was time to take his faith more seriously. A short time later his wife became sick with cancer.

With a sense of urgency, he began looking for resources on divine healing. He found Curry Blake's Divine Healing Technician series and devoured it. With a renewed faith, he sprang into action, and began praying for his wife to be healed. He searched for more material on healing and that's when he found my website. He began reading it and after months of poring over my articles he contacted me. Early in 2012, I received an inquiry from him. He wanted to know if I would consider visiting Australia to teach on healing. I told him I was honored, but that I had no money for such a trip.

A few nights later, I had a dream where I was being sent overseas as an ambassador to establish trade with a small group of people. When I awoke that morning, I found another e-mail from the banker. He offered to pay all of our travel expenses, if we would agree to come to Australia to teach on healing. Taking the dream as confirmation that God wanted me to make the trip, the first order of business was to find out more about this fellow and what he wanted from me. Over the next two months we sent e-mails back and forth and talked over Skype. We had to develop some familiarity with each other, if this venture was going to succeed. And I had some personal issues to deal with.

I'd never traveled overseas before. I'd only taught one class on healing and although it was a success, teaching healing and miracles overseas to a group of strangers was a daunting task. I also worked a full-time job and I had to arrange time off work. At the same time, my wife was trying to find a job. I had to convince her that taking time away from my work, and her efforts to find work, wouldn't put us in a financial bind. After a lot of discussion, we finally agreed to go, though I could tell that my wife was still uneasy about the decision.

After we committed to making the trip, the banker informed us that his wife had come down with terminal cancer. He didn't tell us this until after we made a commitment, because he didn't want to appear desperate and he didn't want our decision to be influenced by emotions. The last thing he wanted was to use pressure or manipulation to get us to come to Australia.

We joined with him in prayer for his wife's healing from a distance. I rallied some friends to pray on her behalf. We all had so much hope that she would be healed. Not long after we began praying, we received news that she had suddenly passed away. My wife was devastated. She spent the entire day crying. The Banker was heartbroken. He spent the following months battling thoughts of depression, hopelessness and despair, wondering what he did wrong in his efforts to get her healed.

Many people would have given up on the teaching trip at this point. His faith for healing was in shambles. I was an unknown person to his circle of friends. He's a very busy man, and now had two children to raise on his own and a demanding full-time job. No one would have blamed him if he pulled the plug on the trip.

But the banker is a man of his word. Once he commits himself to a task, he sees it through to the end, regardless of the consequences to himself or feelings of doubt he has along the way. We made plans to visit Brisbane for two weeks in September. He took a lot of risk in this adventure. The church he's connected to has hosted a number of itinerant preachers, who've been happy to visit for a few days, give an inspiring message, a few prophetic words, and perhaps lay hands on a few people, then leave. And they're never heard from again.

He had a different plan for me. His hope was to bring us to Brisbane to mentor him and his friends in the ways of the supernatural. Not through preaching, but by example. He wanted us to train a group of friends who volunteer with a local church. The church provides them with a van to get from place to place. They set up portable tables where they serve food, coffee, and tea. They pray with the homeless, the drug-addicted, and the mentally ill on the streets. We would ride along in the vans and discuss their concerns, answer their questions, and model the kingdom of God for them. The first week we would ride along on the street vans. The second week, we'd hold meetings where we would train them in prophecy, healing, deliverance and anything else they needed.

The banker also understood the need for relationship in ministry. He wanted to establish a long-term relationship where he and I would share in the work of ministry over many years, so that the seeds we planted would grow into maturity. Reading my blog gave him a lot of insights into what makes me tick. He figured that once we met, we'd get along pretty well and a long-term relationship would follow. His hope was that if he could get me to come to Australia, and if things went well, if we were received by his friends, if healing and miracles were demonstrated and if his friends were able to grow in the supernatural, we would return for a follow-up visit.

Officially, he set his expectations pretty low. He managed the expectations of those around him by simply saying, "Even if only one person gets this... if only one person is touched and learns how much God loves to bless, heal, and restore people, then it will be worth it." He took the view that if we were simply able to encourage his friends with testimonies of healing and build their faith, it would be a successful trip. Anything more would be icing on the cake.

The banker and I have become real friends. I was surprised at how much we have in common. Between days of ministry, he drove us to sightseeing destinations and we talked non-stop everywhere we went. He's quite an amazing fellow. And he's very unlike the stereotype of the greedy banker many of us envision.

When Jesus sent His disciples out, He told them to find a person of peace (see Luke 10:6.) A person of peace, like my friend the banker, is someone who sees the work that God is doing in us. They have a sphere of influence into which they invite us to bring the kingdom of God. They are the door to the harvest field. We are the door to the kingdom of God. Ministry flows through these doors. It's quite simple, really. And I'm finding that it works pretty well.

The next seven stories happened during our trip to Australia in September of 2012.

Are You Crazy – Who Wouldn't Want to Go to Australia?

This is a message my wife wrote about our trip to Australia. She discusses the problems she wrestled with and the ways in which God showed her His faithfulness.

MY HUSBAND AND I HAD many wonderful experiences on our trip to Brisbane, Australia. He asked me to write about a particular series of events surrounding the trip from my perspective because they were events that personally affected my faith. My husband will share stories of some of the amazing supernatural healings we saw, but this is really a story of how I learned to trust the Lord more, especially in the area of financial provision. So if you struggle with trusting God in this area, my hope is that you will be encouraged by the story I am about to tell.

Let me say that there was no way we would have made this trip without God providing a way. I had been unemployed and our household funds were very tight when the trip was first proposed. However, I really did believe it was God's will that my husband would go to Brisbane to minister and teach on healing.

The trip was generously funded by the banker. As time moved along, the plans for our trip were coming together more easily than I expected. I saw it as an open door and an awesome opportunity for my husband, but I was not so sure it was God's will that I should go along.

I don't consider myself to be a spiritual giant. I wasn't convinced I had anything spiritually significant to offer others on the trip, except my prayers. My husband wanted me to go, but I secretly kept hoping the whole thing would fall apart, so I could stay home in my comfort zone.

Here's what was going through my mind:

"I don't like long plane rides."

"I am unworthy."

"I wonder what will be expected of me."

"We won't be earning money while we're gone."

I expressed my reluctance to my husband… often. Finally, I started to become more vocal with others about not wanting to go. The reaction I got from people was, "Are you crazy? Who wouldn't want to go to Australia?"

Although I consider myself to be a ministry partner with my husband, I've leaned toward the notion that it is really *his* ministry and *his* calling to heal the sick. I'm there to support, love, and encourage him. I'm very good at that part. My talents are different than my husband's and I had this sense that my true destiny was not fully known to me yet. My husband told me that God had spoken my destiny clearly to me (mainly through dreams and prophetic words) but I hadn't trusted that I was hearing Him correctly. I didn't trust myself to walk it out, or I didn't trust God enough to bring it to pass.

First a little background: I was raised without God and lived as an atheist for about 40 years. I scoffed at believers and didn't understand a single thing about faith, nor did I want to. But then, I gave my life to Jesus in 1998 during a defining moment in my unbelieving life: my second divorce. I was so accustomed to doing things in my own strength, and working hard to pay for everything I needed or wanted, that I was never comfortable stepping out to do something if I couldn't see where the money was coming from. My nature is to be responsible, pay our bills on time, and keep a good credit score, etc. Because we would lose some income if we took the trip, I was stressing out about how we were going to pay our bills.

After much grumbling on my part about the trip, my husband finally said, "I really need you to go with me on the trip." Others had encouraged me by reminding me that we are indeed a team, and I do have something to offer, even if I don't realize it. I didn't want to let my husband down or disobey God when He clearly made a way for this to happen. So I finally settled it in my mind; I needed to bite the bullet and go.

Before the trip, I decided to set up our household bills to be paid automatically while we were gone so we wouldn't be late with payments. I needed to project the amount of income we could expect from my husband's vacation pay and add up all the bills and expenses. As I filled out the amounts in a spreadsheet, my projections showed our account would be short. It would go into a negative balance! There wouldn't be enough money to pay everything because my husband wouldn't be paid any overtime wages while we were gone.

I had been unemployed for about ten months and his overtime pay had been vital to make ends meet, so I really went into panic mode. In fact, never in my life have I broken out in hives from stress (or anything else) but this deficit news was just enough to send my body over the edge with a case of hives.

While I was fretting and losing sleep, my husband tried to soothe my fears telling me, "You just have to trust that God will make a way and provide what we need. He wouldn't ask us to go to Australia if He wasn't going to provide everything we need." He was so full of faith, and I was so skeptical. It further deepened my thinking that I really had nothing to offer anyone. My faith was so small.

Fear is the opposite of faith. I knew that. I felt worse, and quite guilty for not having the faith. "Why doesn't He provide *all* the money ahead of time so I don't have to freak out and worry?" I asked.

"Well," said my husband, "That wouldn't require faith, would it?"

"Ugh," I said.

The gears in my brain began working overtime. How could I guarantee that the funds would be there while we were gone, so I wouldn't have to worry through the whole trip? We had already built up some credit card debt when we moved to Arizona, and it was a struggle trying to pay that down while I was without a job.

My clever credit card company sent me some checks to entice me into more debt at 0% interest for a year. I didn't want to add more debt by using one of the checks, but I didn't see any other way to get fast cash into our account just days before the trip. So, I wrote one of those credit card checks to myself and deposited $1000 into our account to cover any deficit for the month.

Sigh... I wasn't exactly relieved. I still wondered how we would pay it back. But at least I could put off the problem for now and try to stop fretting about it. So we packed our bags and flew across the Pacific Ocean. When we arrived, we were greeted at the airport just before dawn by our host, the banker.

For the first couple of days in Brisbane, we worked with local street van teams that deliver food to the homeless. Throughout our trip, the banker drove us around and generously paid for our expenses. As I said, we couldn't have done this without divine help and someone like him, who was obedient to what God wanted to do.

Meeting the street van teams was great and it was inspiring to serve beside them. The Access van volunteers were so dedicated to serving hurting and unfortunate people. For many years, they have been faithfully preparing sandwiches and heating up meat pies in a small church kitchen to distribute to the needy. They heat water in a huge urn for coffee, tea, and Milo. Then they pack it all up in the vans and go out on pre-planned routes to shelters—even under bridges where homeless people gather. This could be particularly dangerous, if not for the Lord's protection.

We prayed for folks and saw some healings right away. My husband and I spoke at a small church in Darra. I really didn't know what was expected of me, but somehow, God stepped in and gave me the words I needed to say. My husband took the lead, teaching about healing. We both laid hands on many sick and hurting people throughout our two-week stay. I gave a testimony of my two failed marriages, a rape at knife-point when I was 19, and how the Lord modeled forgiveness to me many years after that event. Some women came up to me afterwards and said, "Your testimony really helped me." They told me their stories and asked for prayer. I was beginning to see that I did have a purpose on this trip.

On the third day, our host drove us to his lovely country home to spend some more time with his mum and the kids. He stopped at his mailbox before entering the driveway and pulled out a few envelopes. There was an envelope addressed to my husband and myself. I was very surprised. Who would send us a letter in Australia? How did they know where we were staying?

When we got into the house, I saw the return address. It was from a friend who lives in Perth. She was one of my husband's Facebook friends for a long time, but more recently she began sending me encouraging emails about a health issue I'd been struggling with. We had never met this lovely woman. Perth is on the western coast of the country. We were in Brisbane, on the eastern coast. We wanted to meet up with her and other Facebook acquaintances from Perth, but were not able to do it on this trip.

My husband handed me the envelope. It didn't feel like a letter. It was a padded envelope. Inside was a lovely necklace with two pearl pendants that could be switched out, one dark pearl and one white pearl. "Awww... this is so nice," I said. I couldn't believe she was sending me a gift. I think it's hard to choose jewelry for someone you don't know, but this piece actually fit my style. I thought that in itself, was amazing.

There were two smaller decorative envelopes inside the padded envelope. One said "Letter" so I opened it. Her letter started with these words "You are on your way to Brisbane as I write this."

She wrote:

> *"I had been planning to come and meet up with you but when I noticed your itinerary was only for a couple of weeks, I realized with birthday commitments I had, it wasn't going to work. I was disappointed. I could still come, but it would have only been for a few days and it was a long way for a short visit. I don't believe it was meant to be."*

She wrote three lovely pages to us, including scriptures that the Lord was bringing to her attention, (Colossians 3:1-2 and 1 Corinthians 2: 9-16.) She asked us to send her a message to let her know the envelope arrived safely. At the end of the letter, she mentioned something about wanting to buy us an iPad. She said, "... so use this money for this."

Amazingly, the last envelope inside the padded outer envelope contained a stack of Australian bills. It was quite a thick stack of 50 dollar bills. In fact, standing with the banker at the counter in his kitchen, we all knew it was way more than an iPad would cost. I started to count it, but stopped after I got to about $500 because I was so overwhelmed.

So, we put it aside for a while and our host let us use his phone to call her. We thanked her for the gift and the money and told her how surprised we were. We got a chance to talk about spiritual things and how the trip was going. She shared the story of how God directed her in all this. Here's how it happened:

> *The Lord asked me to put away a bit of grocery money every fortnight over a period of time. I wasn't sure what He wanted me to use it for. When I heard you were coming to Brisbane, I wanted to bless you and thought it would be nice to send about $250. But the Lord spoke to me and said "Send it all."*
>
> *I didn't hesitate, I wanted to be obedient. God had never asked me to give a sum this large to anyone before. I knew I was hearing from Him, so there was no question in my mind that I needed to send it... but how?*

I couldn't transfer the money through electronic banking because I didn't have an account with that capability. I asked a few friends if they would deposit my cash and transfer the money to you. No one wanted to help me with that; they didn't think I should send money to people I'd never met in person.

So in a big step of faith, I put the whole stack of cash in an envelope, tucked it inside the padded envelope and put regular postage on it. Then, the Lord told me to put it in the express box. I didn't have express postage on the envelope, and told God I couldn't do it. After trying to reason with Him several times, He assured me that it would be okay. He wanted the money to arrive quickly. So I dropped it in the express box.

When we ended our phone call with her, we went back to the envelope and curiously began counting the money. We got to 500, then 600, and were still counting. The final count was $1000. The exact amount that I had transferred into our account to cover our shortfall before we left! I immediately said to my husband, "Why do I ever doubt God?" Then my eyes filled with tears.

So, through an obedient and faithful servant, the Lord showed me that He understood my fears about the finances, that He saw my distress, and that He had it covered the whole time. Let me say, she knew nothing about my financial worries. My husband and I were the only ones who knew about it. We were hoping God would help us pay back the $1000, but He moved in advance of our arrival in Brisbane. I believe He wanted the money to get to us quickly so that I wouldn't continue fretting about it. And He wanted to show me that He is my provider. I will always have this testimony of how He provided for me. And she will always have this amazing testimony of how God used her to provide an exact amount to meet the specific need of a friend.

Most of us have heard stories of the Lord asking someone to give, and it turned out to be the exact amount that the person needed who was receiving it. He has asked me to give specific amounts to different individuals at times, but I never got confirmation that it was the exact amount they needed. I'd been striving to work for everything in my life for so long. I lacked faith in the area of provision; this was a weakness in my walk with Him. But it's true. His strength is perfected in our weakness.

After that, I was challenged to do the things He was nudging me to do, the things I had been afraid to do because of the economy or my jobless situation. Instead of applying for more unemployment compensation, I started my own business at home. As I step into His purpose, He blesses the work and meets my needs.

Wait, there's more!

Months before we left for Australia, I was trying to pay down some credit card debt and looked at my bill wondering why the amount we owed was getting larger instead of smaller. I had not made any purchases for months. I checked my statements and saw a $75 charge that was being added each month. It looked like a service I had signed up for, but I'd forgotten what it was. I figured I should call them and cancel it. So I called the toll-free number and I told them I wanted to cancel their service because I was currently unemployed.

The gentleman on the phone said, "You're unemployed? Ma'am, this charge is for insurance that pays your monthly credit card payment if you get laid off or are unemployed."

After he said that, I began to have vague recollection of signing up for this a long time ago. He asked me some questions and said, "It seems as though you will qualify for benefits, but I need you to fill out some paperwork."

He sent me a claim form and I filled in all the details, attached some other documents, and saw that I needed a signature from the last company I worked for. I e-mailed my supervisor. She said she couldn't sign the form. I called the insurance company. They told me I must have the signature from my last employer. I called the employer's corporate office and asked if someone there would sign the form. She told me to fax the papers to them, so I did. I waited and waited, and after a few days I called again, but got their voice-mail. I e-mailed them but they didn't reply.

At this point I was getting discouraged and figured this would be the insurance company's chance to deny me the benefits. I submitted other pieces of information in lieu of the signature, but it was rejected. Days before we left for Australia I called again and finally spoke with someone at the corporate office who said she would help. I faxed everything again. She signed the forms and faxed them back to me... finally. So I mailed everything to the credit card insurance company. They said it would be about ten days before I would get their decision by mail.

When I got back from Australia, there was a letter in my mailbox that said my claim had been accepted and they would make my next credit card payment. We finally saw some progress, but I wished I had put my claim in ten months prior, when I was first laid off. They could have been paying that bill for me all that time. Anyway, I decided to be grateful. The payments would be made as long as I was still unemployed.

After a few days, my credit card bill came. Upon examination, I saw that the insurance company had paid the bills retroactive, back to the date I was first unemployed. Not only did they pay my regular payment amount—they made ten months of DOUBLE monthly payments and also refunded the $75 insurance fee for all ten months! My new balance owed on the card was now HALF of what it was before I went to Australia.

What do you think? Was I just so smart for buying insurance, or was this a blessing of divine debt reduction? After what happened to us with the Australia trip, I'm choosing to see it as His blessing.

Yesterday, Today, and Tomorrow

FOR 19 YEARS, THE PEOPLE at Access Church have been sending teams into the streets of Brisbane to minister to those who are less fortunate. The teams visit hostels, half-way homes, and other locations where the poor and mentally ill live. We arrived and went to work with the crew making sandwiches, heating up meat pies, and filling containers with sweets like doughnuts. The teams also serve hot coffee, Milo, and tea. After preparing the food, we loaded it into a van and set off.

Our first stop was a hostel for abused women and children. We set up two portable tables in the parking lot, put out the food, said a prayer over it, and then began handing it out. A middle-aged woman named Debra stood next to a beautiful tree; the glow of the street light illuminated its tricolored flowers. I asked Debra what kind of plant it was.

"It's called yesterday, today, and tomorrow." She drew my attention to the white flower and said, "This one's yesterday." Pointing to a light purple petal, she said, "This one is today". Pointing at the dark purple one she said, "And this one is tomorrow."

I thanked her and asked if she had any pain in her body that she wanted to have healed.

"I have pain in my back and a lot of sadness. I had three people in my family die from cancer."

"Would it be alright if I prayed with you?"

"I'd be grateful if you did."

I placed my hand in the small of her back. "Holy Spirit, bring your healing touch to Debra. Pain, I command you to leave." I asked if she felt anything.

"It feels like electricity going up and down my spine."

"That's usually a good sign. Why don't you try to touch your toes?"

She reluctantly agreed, thinking the chronic pain would make it difficult. But she put her hands to the ground with ease. A look of shock came over her when she realized she was healed. We prayed for healing of her emotions and the power of God began to work in her mind and heart. His presence made it hard for her to remain standing so one of the team slipped in behind her and prevented her from falling to the ground.

We talked with Debra for quite a while afterward, sharing our experiences and giving her tips on how to keep her healing. My wife and I gave her a hug before we helped the crew load the van. It was time to go to another location. During the first two nights, we saw a number of people healed of chronic pain. We had a blast watching God display His power and love to these wonderful people.

A Sovereign Miracle at Pindary

BEFORE WE LEFT FOR AUSTRALIA, a friend gave us a prophetic word suggesting that God wanted to do things we'd never seen before. Tonight, we made sandwiches, pies, and sausage rolls and loaded the van for another evening on the streets with the less fortunate citizens of Brisbane.

The vans generally stop at three locations each night. The stops might be shelters for the homeless, a city park where natives live in tents, or a home for men just released from prison. One of our stops tonight was at Pindary—a Salvation Army shelter for homeless men. We distributed food, tea, coffee, and Milo and talked with the men about their lives. One benefit of visiting shelters frequently is that you can develop relationships that allow you to mentor the people you meet.

About fifteen minutes after we'd arrived, my host motioned me toward him. He explained that one of the men had a painful toothache. Reacting out of habit I asked, "Can I pray with you?"

"I'd be keen to have someone pray with me."

I placed my hand on his shoulder. "Spirit of pain, I command you to leave. Infection and inflammation get out." After a minute or so of prayer, I asked if he felt any pain.

"It doesn't hurt at all, mate. Hasn't hurt since you got here."

Somewhat confused, I began asking questions. "What do you mean it hasn't hurt since we got here?"

"I had real bad pain in my tooth. I first noticed it yesterday. You blokes showed up, and I was watching as you set up the tables. I noticed something different when you got here. There was a kind presence around you. Hard to describe exactly. Anyway, as I was standing beside you, I noticed my toothache was gone.

"Wait a minute. Are you telling me you felt something different when got here?"

"That's exactly what I'm sayin'. There's a kind of peaceful spirit you have around you and I felt it as soon as you got out of the van."

"And you believe your toothache was healed by standing next to me?"

"That's it, mate."

I asked if he was certain of this story. He insisted that's exactly what happened. We spoke with him and the others about the goodness of a God who would heal a man's toothache before anyone could pray with him. The sovereign miracle allowed God and His goodness to be the focus of our conversation the rest of the night.

Martin's Story

TONIGHT WE VISITED A HOMELESS shelter near the top of a hill in Brisbane. As we handed out food and made coffee, I saw a man approaching. He had a noticeable limp. I introduced myself. "What's your name sir?"

"I go by Martin."

"Nice to meet you, Martin. I couldn't help but notice you were limping."

"Oh that. Doc says I have a torn cruciate ligament. I need surgery."

"Has anyone prayed for you to be healed yet?"

"Lots of people, but it's not any better."

Feeling a little bold I said, "No worries, Martin. We'll have it good as new before we leave."

I asked a couple of team members named Sylvie and Marie to come over and lay hands on him. For the next five minutes they conducted warfare on the injured knee and he began to feel heat. I joined them and eventually all of his knee pain was gone. The only issue left was a clicking sound coming from just under his kneecap. "Martin, I'd like to offer you a choice. We can keep praying and try to get the clicking to leave, or you can rest in the healing you already have and check on it in the morning. I believe the clicking will be gone by morning."

"I'm happy with what you've done already. Reckon I'll see what happens tonight." Since I was speaking at a meeting he planned to attend in a few days, we could follow up with him then.

Martin began to tell the group about some unusual things that have happened to him. He related a story about a friend who had a relative who had just been seen in the emergency department. The doctor was very concerned about his condition. "I says to him, 'don't worry mate, he's gonna be released from the hospital soon.' A few minutes later, he gets a call saying he just went home with a clean bill of health."

He told another story about a roommate who went to the store. "When my mate was leaving, I pulled out a twenty and handed it to him. He said he didn't need it, because he didn't plan to buy much, but I insisted he take it. He was stopped leaving the store and had in his possession a few things he didn't pay for. They were valued at 19 dollars. They were gonna arrest him for shoplifting if he couldn't pay for the items, so he handed over the twenty I gave him and walked home."

Next he told us about a dream he had. In the dream he was sleeping on a table in his yard when a shepherd approached and spoke with him.

The shepherd said, "Martin, I want you to write a book."

"What's the book going to be about?"

The shepherd said, "You."

"What's the title going to be?"

The shepherd replied "Why?" He then said, "Many people will read your book and be saved."

Martin is at the shelter because of a drinking problem. And even though he struggles to maintain sobriety, he has an amazing gift of revelation about the things that happen to people around him and what God is doing in those circumstances. I encouraged him to begin writing down all the stories he could remember and hang onto them. At some point in the future, if he obeyed the shepherd's instructions, God would provide an editor and a publisher to help him write his book.

The Three Monkeys

DURING OUR FINAL MEETING IN Darra, there was a lot of interest in dreams, so before leaving, we spent about an hour discussing dream interpretation with the group. A number of people had been physically healed that week after evil spirits had been cast out, so we also taught a bit more on deliverance. We wrapped up with a discussion on what it means to make disciples.

I met a man named Roland Williamson, who authors the blog *Australian Miracles*, which is devoted to reporting the miraculous works of God in Australia and other places. He sent me a friend request on Facebook and we agreed to meet at a coffee shop where Christians hang out called *The Three Monkeys*. We talked for an hour or so about our common interests.

As we left the coffee shop, we met a group of women who were also leaving. One of them used a cane to walk. I figured it was a divine set-up so I got the woman's attention. "Excuse me, but can I ask why you're walking with a cane?"

"I have a torn meniscus in my knee."

"Can I pray for you?"

"That would be very kind of you."

I placed my hand on her knee. "Spirit of pain, I command you to leave. Meniscus, be made brand new. Inflammation, leave in the name of Jesus." I asked what she felt.

"It feels the same." I prayed two more times and asked how it felt.

"There's a little less pain, but not much." Pointing to her mum, she said, "You really need to pray for her."

I shook her mum's hand and asked her name. "And what do you need to be healed of?"

"I've got a bad shoulder. I can hardly move it at all."

"How would you like to be healed?"

"I'd be delighted."

I placed my hands lightly on her shoulder. Spirit of pain, I command you to leave. Ligaments, cartilage, muscles, bone, nerves and tendons, be healed in the name of Jesus." I asked how she felt.

"I think it's a little better."

I repeated the process two more times and asked how she felt. She extended her arm out then moved it in a circle. She had full range of motion without pain.

The healing gave us an opportunity to speak with the group about the goodness of God and the things He's been doing in Brisbane. A few of them had been burned by religion in the past, but the healing allowed us to focus on the love, mercy, and compassion of God. The realization that they were loved removed the walls they had built against religion. The demonstration of power testified to the truth of God's love, and that truth began to change their hearts.

The Banker's Mum

WHEN TRAVELING FOR PLEASURE, WE generally eat whatever pleases us. One of the perils of traveling for ministry is found in the command of Jesus to remain in the home where you find a person of peace and eat what they put before you (see Luke 10:6-7). This command wouldn't bother me so much were in not found smack in the middle of the rest of his instructions to the disciples, where he told them to heal the sick.

I'm not a big fan of religious legalism, but I think God honors our obedience, when we obey from a heart of love. On this trip, I really wanted to obey the command to eat what was put before me. I've been a picky eater my entire life, but I'm trying to be more open to different types of food.

Earlier in the week, my host introduced me to Vegemite. He was gracious and allowed me to smear it lightly on a piece of toast instead of putting on a thick layer. It wasn't all that bad. I ate the entire piece of toast, which impressed him. Knowing this was our first trip to Australia, he wanted to expose us to the richness of an authentic Aussie dinner. So he bought a kangaroo roast, some herbs and vegetables, and asked his mum to make dinner for us.

His mum is an excellent cook. The veggies were delightful. She did a decent job with the kangaroo roast, though I prefer meat with a little more fat, and kangaroo is extremely lean. The flavor was a bit wild, as you might expect. I noticed that the Banker didn't eat more than a few pieces of the roo roast. I followed suit and threw in the towel after I ate my third piece. After dinner, we got comfortable and had a chat about the miracles we'd seen that week. The Banker's mum told us that she has degenerative joint disease in her spine, which causes her vertebrae to click and pop when she moves. "Maybe we should get you healed," I replied.

I placed my hand on her back. "Holy Spirit, bring your presence. Spirit of pain, I command you to leave. Bones of the spine, come into alignment in the name of Jesus. Inflammation, I command you to leave. Joints, be healed. Discs, be healed. Ligaments, be healed." I asked what she felt.

"It's getting warm."

I prayed again and asked what she felt. "Now it's very warm."

I hugged her and with a smile, gave her my usual line, "You're healed, now stop being a sissy." She hugged me back and thanked me for praying with her. On the follow-up visit, a week later, she reported that the popping and clicking was gone. Because we put up with roo roast the week before, she decided to treat us to a slow-roasted lamb dinner. It was delicious. Sometimes obedience can be a blessing.

The Ticket Agent

As I sat at the gate waiting to board the plane, I carefully wound an elastic bandage around my lower leg, starting just above my toes, working my way upward toward my knee. Having suffered swollen feet from the 15-hour flight to Brisbane two weeks earlier, we stopped at a pharmacy and picked up a few elastic bandages. Just before boarding, we wrapped our feet and lower legs figuring it might prevent swelling on the return flight. My wife and I chatted on the plane, reflecting on the miracles God had done in Australia. We marveled at how He'd connected us to so many wonderful people.

We arrived in Los Angeles and had almost six hours before our connecting flight to Phoenix departed. We negotiated the maze, going from one building to another in search of our gate. On the way, we stopped to talk with a ticket agent. I chose her because she had an immobilizer on her forearm. She was strategically positioned where I could talk with her for a few minutes.

"Hi there. Can I ask you a question?"

With a big smile she said, "You certainly may!"

"What happened to your arm?"

She's an agent at one of the busiest airports in the world. She expects strangers to ask about arrivals, departures, and gate locations. She blushed and began laughing when I hit her with an unexpected question. "Oh, it's just a little shoulder injury." She didn't say why she had an immobilizer on her forearm instead of something around her shoulder, but I didn't ask about it. I knew she needed to help more customers, and I only had a few minutes of her time.

"I was wondering if you'd like to have your shoulder healed."

"I might. But it depends on what you have in mind."

"Nothing dangerous, I promise. I just want to pray with you."

"Pray with me? I'd really like that!"

I placed my hand gently on her shoulder. "Spirits of pain and infirmity, I command you to leave. Ligaments, bones, tendons, muscles, cartilage and nerves, be healed in the name of Jesus." I asked if she felt anything.

"I sure do. My whole arm is tingling."

"The tingling is the power of God healing you."

"Jesus is so good to us, isn't he?" She asked.

"He sure is." We asked where we could find our gate.

With a grateful smile, she said, "Take this escalator behind me to the next level and when you get to the top, make a right. Your gate will be about halfway down on the left."

This meeting took about three minutes from beginning to end. In just three minutes, a complete stranger felt the power and love of God touch her. I'd say it was time well spent.

Ten Minutes

AFTER RETURNING FROM OUR TRIP to Australia, I went straight back to working my regular shift on the ambulance. As we pushed the gurney to our next patient's room, I noticed a tall nurse with black hair limping down the hall with an immobilizer on her foot. My partner went into the patient's room. I went on my mission. I approached the nurse, introduced myself and asked the usual question.

"May I ask what happened to your foot?"

"Oh... I broke it."

"Have you had surgery yet?"

"I was hoping I wouldn't need surgery. The plan was for it to heal on its own. But it's been a slow process."

"Would you like to be healed right now?"

She smiled. "I'd love to be healed. What do you have in mind?"

"I'd like to pray with you."

"Well, of course you can pray with me. I never say no to prayer!"

I bent down and laid my hand on the black plastic immobilizer on her foot. "Spirit of pain, leave. Holy Spirit, bring your presence. Ligaments, nerves, bones, tendons, and muscles, be healed in the name of Jesus. Do you feel anything going on in your foot?"

"No... not really."

I would normally pray a second and a third time, but I had to get back to my patient. "I believe your foot is healed. I think you'll notice the pain leaving in a little while."

"Thank you so much for praying for me."

I went back to my patient, who was a quadriplegic with a tracheostomy.

He had many personal items going along with him on the transport that had to be put into bags, so getting him ready took about ten minutes. Once everything was loaded on the gurney, we headed for the elevator.

On the way to the elevator, I saw the woman with the immobilizer again. She looked at me as I passed by and said, "What did you do to me? My foot feels great!"

"Why don't you test it out and see if there's any pain?"

She stomped her foot on the floor a couple of times. There wasn't any pain. She was completely healed and utterly stunned. I gave her some basic instruction on how to keep her healing and she asked for my name. "I'm going to call your supervisor and tell him how nice it is that they allow you to pray with people."

While this kind of activity might cause you to lose your job in other parts of the world, in the United States, we're blessed to have the freedom to pray on the job, and sometimes we're even commended for it.

I could have assumed this woman was not going to be healed, because nothing happened after I prayed with her the first time. But ten minutes later, she was completely healed. Don't develop the habit of thinking that people aren't healed, just because you don't see an immediate change. This kind of thing happens often enough that I sometimes tell people, "You may not feel anything now, but you will feel it later."

I'd like to propose a challenge: The next time you see someone at work hobbling along with some type of injury, offer to pray with them and watch what happens.

Divine Appointment

I FREQUENTLY FIND MYSELF ON a late call after my scheduled shift is over. Part of being a paramedic is surrendering your time to your patients and your employer who may need a few extra hours now and then. I used to complain about being held over, but I'm not as bitter about it as I once was, thanks to a perspective that my wife shared with me.

Shortly after I began my current job, I found out I was going to be held over a lot. My employer has a policy that permits a two-hour hold-over and they use it nearly every day. I got in the habit of texting my wife to let her know when I would be late. I'd come home and tell her about my day: how many patients we transported, if I prayed with anyone, and if anyone was healed. One day, as I told her about a suicidal patient we transported that I prayed with, she said, "Honey, I know there's always a good reason when you're late. Have you noticed that every time you're held over on a late call, there's someone you get to pray with or encourage? God gives you divine appointments and I'm okay with it."

I'd never considered that. And of course, she was right. When I thought back on the kind of people we transported after the end of our shift, it was almost always someone who needed a touch from God. Today was no exception.

We transported a 64-year-old woman who had weakness in her right leg for two weeks. She didn't think much of it, but she went to see her primary care doctor who did some blood tests, and ordered a CT scan to be done the following week. The results from the scan came back, but her doctor didn't tell her what was wrong. He told her to go to an

Emergency Department and have them evaluate her. So she did. The Emergency Department doctor discovered that she had a large brain tumor. We were transporting her to another hospital for neurosurgery.

We got her loaded in the ambulance and began transporting her. The freeways were jammed with traffic, so we took surface roads. She seemed too happy to be a person who just found out she had a brain tumor. I began to wonder if she even knew about it. On a hunch that perhaps they didn't tell her about it, and being concerned that if I mentioned the word "tumor" she might panic, I decided to find out what she knew.

"So exactly what did they say was wrong with you?"

"Well... they said I had some kind of lesion in my brain." She said, without a trace of worry in her voice.

Awesome, I thought to myself. They lied to her. Well, not technically of course, because strictly speaking, a tumor is a kind of lesion. It just happens to be the worst kind, and they didn't feel like telling her about it. Life is just easier when you hide those unpleasant details from people. I got a set of vitals, then asked my next question.

"Do you believe in divine appointments?"

She looked at me with a smile and replied, "Well... I guess so."

"So do I and I think you're having one right now." I told her about some of the people I'd seen healed including a couple of people with tumors. "Can I pray with you to be healed?"

"I'd like that."

I placed my hand on her shoulder, commanded the "lesion" to be gone, told demons to hit the road and asked the Holy Spirit to bring His presence and touch her. She didn't feel anything and our mobile CT scanner was in the shop for repairs, so I don't know if she was healed. But I know she was blessed. And sometimes that's enough.

The Helicopter Dream

———⊙⊗⊗⊙———

In 2012, I BEGAN WRITING stories about my past and sharing them publicly. I wrote them for several reasons. One was that I needed to be healed from the fear of what people would think about me if they ever found out about my past.

With the help of my friends Robin Demer, Heather Goodman, Deonna Crochet, and Craig Adams, I finally dragged the skeletons out of my closet and dealt with the fear and insecurity once and for all. Instead of the rejection I expected, I found people drawing even closer to me. It was a very liberating experience.

I suspected that if I opened up about my past, other people would too, but I didn't anticipate the degree to which it would happen. After I began writing about the troubles I'd had (mostly involving failed relationships) dozens of friends began discussing their past, and many of them began to receive healing of rejection, shame, and guilt. Some even started support groups. But one story in particular touched me more than any other. It involved a dream from God that was given to a woman I didn't know named Sara.

In the dream, Sara saw a rescue helicopter hovering above her town. She knew that the helicopter came to deliver an important message, but she didn't know what the message was. In the dream, she heard conversations with a grieving girl who was healed emotionally, and as the transformation on the inside of this girl occurred, she was changed on the outside.

After she had the dream, Sara began looking for the helicopter image and when she got to my Facebook page, she realized it was the same one from her dream. She sent me a private message sharing her dream, and asked if I could help her interpret it. I didn't have a good interpretation of the dream, but we kept in touch over the next few weeks.

About a month after her dream, I began writing on my blog about the affair I had in 2005 that ended my first marriage. I wrote that I felt like I'd been emotionally abandoned by my wife and that I knew that my actions had destroyed the trust of my daughter.

My blog post prompted Sara to send me another private message:

Wow, I read your post today. My dad did something similar when I was your daughter's age. I remember the shock of it, up until that day I always wanted to marry a man just like my dad. What your post made me think was, wow, he had a side of the story too. He was probably tormented too. He probably felt terrible too.

I read your post and just felt respect for your courage to expose yourself. I felt mercy towards you, felt like you deserved grace. And you're a stranger. Shouldn't those things be extended first to a loved one? Like my own father?... how in the world did it take 18 years to realize his decision wasn't personal? It was his own mistake, not made intentionally to hurt those he loved, just an attempt to find something HE was missing.

The truth shall set you free, interesting that truth is a person too. Liberating to realize sometimes we need to be set free from other people's bad decisions because it was never about us anyway.

Thank you.
Sara

During her parents' divorce, all Sara could see was her father's selfishness. She couldn't see his pain or loneliness. She had no empathy for him and never considered his side of the story, until she read my story. She realized that she needed to forgive her father and let the mistakes of the past be healed.

God has used my story to touch the hearts of a lot of people in ways I never imagined. That doesn't excuse my sins. I did some terrible things that can never be justified. But when we're willing to talk about our mistakes in a desire to be healed of the shame, guilt, and anger they can bring, there is healing for ourselves and for others.

Reply to the Helicopter Dream:

A short time later, I received another private message from Sara. She wanted to share a little more about the dream and her thoughts on how God set things up:

Sorry about the slow response, I really wanted to write how this had all gone down, I'm glad you shared it. I'm currently on a "Facebook fast" but when I saw this in my e-mail I had to check it out. I could tell you held back a little, just unsure of what to share. So if you want, here's the full version from my perspective.

A few months back I had a dream. I awoke in my house to find small flames everywhere. The walls, floor, etc. I was alarmed at first, thinking my house is on FIRE! I quickly realized these flames were contained and not spreading. I looked out my window to see them outside too, so I went into my front yard (which, as I say this, I realize could represent my future? Front yard/future? Duh.)

I could see these little flames all over my property and all the way to town. (We live 14 miles out of town in western Nebraska.) I feel the urge to get to town as a rescue helicopter flies into the scene. I literally hear that it's carrying a message that's really important that I need to remember. It hovers and I see LAM 10:15 on the side of the chopper. I assume that is the message and focus intently on what that could mean. The chopper flies off and all the sudden I'm back in my house.

I see a mirror in the living room that's full length, and I'm hesitant to walk to it. I do anyway and see a reflection of a young girl—in her pre-teen years who is crying and upset. She keeps crying and talking but I can't understand what she's saying. She starts to transform physically. I compare it to a meth-makeover advertisement you see on the billboards but instead of going from good to worse, the reflection gets better and better.

Physically, the girl is transforming but as she's changing, the tears are leaving and the sadness and grief are too. There is a healing taking place on the inside so profound it's affecting her physical appearance on the outside. I never do understand a word the reflection says, but as she's changed, a normalcy returns to her image and she's at peace. Then I wake up.

My obvious reaction was the message that I was supposed to remember was whatever the helicopter was bringing. Upon my daily

Facebook check I scroll across a picture of the medic chopper on Praying Medic's site and realize THAT'S THE CHOPPER from my dream! I focused on the LAM 10:15 for weeks thinking it was a Bible verse or some coded answer to something the Holy Spirit is trying to speak to me. I prayed, I sought interpretation, all to no avail. Until one day I see Praying Medic has a post about his life story.

I start reading about his affair, his emotions, his turmoil, his raw desires, his regret, his pain. His torture somehow spoke to a side of me I didn't know needed to be spoken to. I related to his daughter, who he was close to, and who then had her world ripped out from under her feet.

A mere week or two before I found out what my dad had done, I remembered thinking how great he was, how lucky I was, how I wanted to find a guy just like him someday. Then, in a blink of an eye, that pedestal I put him on was incinerated and my life was flipped upside down. Somehow, I could never see things from his perspective. I thought to be able to do something like that, he must not have loved us at all. I thought all the times he was good, must have been a lie. All the times he pretended to care, were fake. Because you certainly couldn't run your family through a shredder like he had if you cared at all. That's what I thought.

Then, warp-speed 18 years forward and I'm reading a post from a person who's done almost the same thing. But I hear his heart. Through adult lenses I realize what he did was just for himself. Not an intentional attack to crush his children and wife. I empathized with his pain, and saw his heart. He did what he did to fill some void inside. It's really that simple. It didn't mean he didn't regret it, it didn't mean he didn't love his kids enough, it just meant he made a mistake.

As I'm reading the post I'm bawling like a baby. Reliving my event, I'm realizing sometimes we get caught in the crossfire of other people's mistakes, but those mistakes aren't about us. That arrow wasn't intended for us, it just happened to hit where it hurts. Forgiveness allows us to release OURSELVES from other people's mistakes.

Sitting at a computer on Facebook, I realized the message the Medic helicopter would bring was one I wouldn't even know I was looking for. One of forgiveness and a realization that we have a Father—a good and perfect one. He never lets us down. He makes no mistakes. He's safe to put on a pedestal. He comes with a message of perfect love and wants us all to experience that. When we can set our gaze onto that, somehow the actions and mistakes of the ones around us seem a little less important, seem a little more forgivable, and that's His grace. It frees the person who made a mistake or maybe just the one caught in the crossfire. It frees us all. Amazed, humbled, and awed at the Holy Spirit's intricate set of events, seemingly random and unconnected, that heals and transform in a way only a perfect Father can.

My deepest thanks to you and your family, Praying Medic. For putting yourself on the chopping block and having the courage to face whatever came. There is healing that can only come from honesty and forgiveness. I found mine, and it is my sincere prayer you all have found yours. I guess He really can turn a mess into a message can't He?

I realized there were parts of the dream I had condensed out of my e-mail and wanted you to have the full version I've been intending to send. You don't have to change anything you wrote. It's great. I just wanted you to know the full version of what had taken place. Feel free to share as you like. Thanks again for sharing.

God Bless.
Sara

Fourth Time's a Charm

WHEN WE ARRIVED AT THE nurse's station, the nurse asked us not to go down the hall that was straight ahead. Even though it was the shortest route to our patient's room, she directed us to another hallway that went all the way around the ICU. I had to know why. "So why are we taking the long way around?"

"The patient in that room just died. The chaplain is counseling his family in the hallway outside the room."

Fair enough. We took the long way to our patient's room and met his nurse, who was very friendly, but extremely busy. She was taking care of both my patient and the one who died. While we waited, she discussed the resuscitation attempt of the other patient with one of the doctors. Then she made a phone call and left a message with the answering service for the hospital we were transporting our patient to. I could tell this was going to be an interesting transport.

She came over and apologized for the chaos and told me our patient couldn't be released yet. "I've been calling the receiving hospital for 30 minutes and I can't reach anyone to give them report. Until I'm able to contact someone to give report to, he can't be transported." So the transport was on hold.

She took me aside and gave me the run down on our patient. He was in his early forties and had a history of life-long alcohol abuse, which led to liver failure. The day he was admitted to the hospital, he went into cardiac arrest four times. Each time he coded, they resuscitated him, which left him with a completely broken rib cage. Every time he coughed or took a deep breath you could hear his ribs grating against each other. *Well, I haven't seen that in a long time,* I thought to myself.

His stay in the hospital was chaotic from the start and that's how it remained. When they took him to the cath lab to do the angiogram, there was another patient on the procedure table. He went into cardiac arrest while waiting. When they finally did get him in for his angiogram, they found two completely blocked arteries that could not be stented. They tried to open them with a balloon, but they knew it would only be a matter of time before the arteries closed again. No wonder he coded four times. He was lucky to still be alive.

We were transporting him to another hospital for a liver transplant, and because his heart was in such bad shape, they would need multiple teams in the operating room when they did the transplant if he had any hope of surviving. The nurse tried again to reach the receiving hospital with no luck. We went into his room and introduced ourselves. I explained to my patient, whose name was Steve, that there was a slight delay, but that we'd get him on the road as soon as possible.

Liver failure has got to be one of the worst conditions to live with. Steve's abdomen was swollen to twice the normal size. His skin was yellow from head to toe. Sitting in a chair beside the hospital bed, he looked miserable. I told him what our plan was and asked if his wife would be following us or if she had other plans. "She was hoping she could follow the ambulance in her car," Steve said. We told her that would be fine, as long as she didn't follow us too closely, didn't run a red light trying to keep up with us, and didn't park in the ambulance parking when we got to the other hospital. We quickly killed twenty minutes with small talk. Finally, Steve's nurse came back into the room. She was able to give report to the receiving hospital.

Show time.

We got Steve loaded in the ambulance and I took a seat next to him on the bench. "I'm curious to know if you remember anything from your cardiac arrest."

"I'll tell you everything I can remember." As we rolled through the streets of Phoenix, we talked about his stay in the hospital. "I remember the first time I went into cardiac arrest. I was in the emergency department. I had terrible chest pain then they said my heart stopped. They did CPR on me for a while and broke most of my ribs. Then they shocked me and my heart started beating again. After that they sent me to the ICU. The next morning my heart stopped again.

They started CPR again and shocked a couple of times before I came back. Later that day they sent me to the cath lab but there was a patient in front of me, so I had to wait. My heart stopped again while I was waiting. I survived the cath lab but my heart stopped one more time in the ICU."

"You cheated death four times. That's a pretty amazing feat. Do you remember anything from the times your heart stopped? Any bright lights... going through a tunnel, maybe a meeting with Jesus?"

"No, I don't remember anything like that." I was a little disappointed, but a lot of people don't remember anything from their near-death experiences.

"But I do remember one thing... I was on some heavy duty tranquilizers for a couple of weeks before I came to the hospital. The first three days were a blur except I had what my doctor said were hallucinations. During the days after my heart stopped it seemed like I was in a dream world. There were all these weird creatures and strange looking places like nothing I'd ever seen before. The places I went and things I saw were more real than the world we're in right now. When I became conscious, I talked to my wife about what I saw. She didn't see any of those things, so I wrote it all off as hallucinations."

"Well isn't that interesting?" I replied. I'm beginning to question the understanding we have about hallucinations. It's a thorny subject and I won't unpack it here, but I think we show a lack of understanding when we refer to experiences that other people have, which are not experienced by us, as hallucinations. When I pray, I often see things that no one else sees. Does that mean I'm hallucinating, too?

Okay... back to the story.

Shortly before we arrived, I asked if I could pray for Steve to be healed.

"That would be great," he replied.

I placed my hand on his shoulder. "Lord, I declare your goodness over Steve. He will live and not die. Bring your presence and touch him. I command sickness and disease to leave, in the name of Jesus. Liver and heart be healed."

After I prayed with him, we talked about our destinies. "Steve, I found out a few years ago that my purpose for being here is to pray with people and teach them about God, which is kind of ironic since I've been an atheist for most of my life. I've talked with a lot of people who have stepped into eternity. I'm convinced that very few of us get off this rock before our earthy assignment is complete. If we come back here after we die, there's a reason for it. You have a divine destiny and you need to find out what it is."

"I've thought about that a lot, actually. But I still don't know what my purpose is for being here."

We wheeled Steve to his room and got him off the gurney as gently as we could. Then we helped him into bed. "I don't know what your purpose is for being here, Steve. But God does. You might ask *Him* why you're still here."

It would be an amazing miracle if Steve was healed. But I'll probably never know for sure until I step into eternity when my destiny here is complete.

iPod Dock Healing

SEVERAL YEARS BEFORE MY WIFE and I were married, she was given a Bose iPod docking station from her son as a gift. The docking station is a portable sound system that amplifies your iPod. Bose makes some of the best quality sound equipment and her docking station gets a lot of use. In the summer, we put it out by the pool to bring music outside. It's the only thing we have for listening to music, except our computers.

One day the docking station finally gave up the ghost. It just stopped working. It wouldn't power up. We tried plugging it into different outlets. I took the back off to see if there were any broken wires I might be able to repair, and I did the usual troubleshooting, but it was to no avail. Her beloved iPod dock was toast. (With no Vegemite in sight.) We were pretty bummed out.

A couple of friends, Gwendolyn and Larry, were in the area for a couple of weeks looking for a home. We invited them over and planned a dinner party beside the pool. Gwendolyn is no stranger to the miraculous. She's the one who taught us how to command storms to cease and she's driven her car for hundreds of miles on an empty gas tank. When they arrived, we were getting prepared. My wife took the broken iPod docking station outside and placed it in the stand on the patio, knowing that it didn't work. I didn't think much about it at the time.

We made some margaritas and got comfortable on the patio. Gwen and my wife got to talking and decided it was time to pray over the broken iPod dock so we could have music. I learned later that my wife had this all planned out in her mind. She believed that if, by faith, she brought the docking station outside, plugged it in and had us pray over it, God would repair it. So that's what we did.

The four of us stood in agreement and declared that the docking station would be repaired. While I was praying, I saw a vision of broken electrical wires. So I commanded them to be made new. The others prayed as they were led by the Spirit. After everyone was done praying, my wife walked confidently over and turned the iPod on.

Music came forth. The docking station has worked perfectly since then. We all rejoiced at God's gracious hand and the love He has for His kids. It was a wonderful night of telling Holy Ghost stories and praying for each other's needs.

Hablo Español?

MANUEL TRANSLATED MY QUESTIONS FOR his mother. She would smile and reply to him in a language I didn't understand. "How do you say, 'sign here'?" I asked.

I needed her signature before we could transport Manuel. He told me what to say. I turned to her and said, "firme aquí." She signed her name in the little white box on my laptop computer and we moved Manuel to the gurney. "I really need to learn Spanish," I mumbled to myself.

Manuel's father had just drained the radiator of his truck. He told Manuel not to go near the hot coolant, but 12-year-olds can be curious and his curiosity got the best of him. A few minutes later the coolant spilled on his legs when he got to close to it. We were transporting him to the burn center. The morphine did its job and his pain was bearable so we talked on the way. He complained to his mother about not eating anything all day. His mom said he would be fine. (Well, I think that's what she said.)

"Manuel, I once went 19 days without eating. You're going to be fine."

"Nineteen days, Are you serious?"

"Yeah. But 19 days is nothing. I have friends who have fasted for 40 days." He told his mother and she smiled at me. They talked for a while in Spanish. He asked why I fasted for 19 days.

"So that I could hear God's voice more clearly. The first time I fasted, it was for three days and the second time was for six, then 12, and finally 19 days. Fasting always helps me hear God's voice more clearly."

He told his mom what I said, she replied back, and he translated it for me. It just so happened that she was currently reading a book about fasting and she was a little afraid to try it, but the experiences I shared gave her courage.

Manuel said his mother is a believer, but she fears that he isn't interested in God, because he doesn't talk about Him the way she does. "I do believe in God, but I just don't know much about him." I spent a few minutes telling him healing stories and shared a few dreams with him. He was very interested. Each time I told a story, he told it to his mother in Spanish.

I told him about the woman I prayed with who cut her neck open and about the e-mail I received from her landlord saying that her neck had been healed. "Wow," Manuel said. "I felt something move inside me when you said that!"

His mother wanted to know if I saw angels. I told her I see and hear them at times. Manuel said she is very interested in them. We talked about the supernatural all the way to the hospital. Manuel translated everything I said. He had his mother take a picture of us. He was the second patient that week who posted a picture of themselves with me on Facebook.

Manuel showed more interest in my stories than I expected. He seemed to be hungry for the supernatural. I told him that God is always looking for people who want to see miracles happen. "He wants to touch people who are hurting," I said. "And He'll use anyone to do it. Ask God to teach you how to do this stuff, Manuel. It's not as hard as you think."

We took Manuel inside the burn unit and moved him to the bed. As soon as we had him moved over they began popping the blisters and removing the loose skin from his legs. His mother wanted to know if she could keep in touch with me so I gave her my contact information. That gave me one more reason to learn Spanish. It was a beautiful ending to an amazing shift.

Miracle Car Repair

WE HAD A USED CAR that we bought for our daughter so she could go back and forth to school. It had a lot of miles on it. The car had been running rough for six months, hesitating and stalling at intersections. After finishing her first year of college, she moved out of state, so we didn't need the car anymore, but I didn't want to sell it in that condition. I knew we would get less money if it wasn't running well and I didn't want to sell someone a car that needed repair. I thought I might try fixing it by changing the spark plugs and a replacing few other parts, in the hope that I could get it running better before we sold it. On my way out to the garage to take a look under the hood, I heard the Holy Spirit say, "Didn't I fix the iPod dock?"

(Silence)

I thought, yes, Lord. You sure did.

As I walked to the tool box, I thought to myself, Why not? If He fixed a broken iPod dock, He could make this broken car run like it was supposed to. So I got inside the car, closed the door and started making declarations that the ignition system would work properly and the fuel system would be cleaned out. "Come on Angels! Get to work on this car and make it run, in Jesus' name!"

I prayed over the car and made declarations for three or four minutes. Then I turned the key and drove it down the street. At the first intersection, it accelerated smoothly. I drove it for about ten minutes, going through a lot of intersections. At some intersections, I felt a little fear creep into my mind. I wondered what I would do if it started to hesitate. Sure enough, the car hesitated a little when I became fearful. So I commanded the car to be healed and I kept on driving. I dealt with the fear by imagining the car accelerating smoothly through each intersection. Each time I did this, there was no hesitation.

I drove the car home and told my wife what happened. She didn't believe me, so we went for a drive together. The car drove perfectly and never hesitated once.

So what's the point of all this?

BELIEVE!

Just believe that God wants to fix your broken junk! Believe Him when He tells you things that are outside your grid of understanding. In faith, speak to the junk and command it to work. Get the angels to help you out. They kinda dig miracles and it keeps them busy and entertained. They like to watch unbelief vanish.

And remember, when you're doing the happy dance before the Lord, the angels are dancing with you.

Better Pack a Lunch

SHARON MOVED HERSELF TO THE gurney and began fastening the seat belts. I gave my partner a puzzled look. No one puts the seat belts on themselves. She asked the nurse to hand her the brown paper bag on the counter. "What's in there?" I asked.

"My lunch."

"You brought your own lunch to the hospital?"

"Sure did. Where I'm going, they won't give you any food until after you've been through the intake process and I'm not waiting that long to eat."

Obviously, this wasn't her first rodeo. As we rolled her toward the door, she talked about her previous trips to the mental health treatment facility. She'd been there many times. That's why she brought her lunch. After we got her loaded, she filled me in on the events that brought her to the emergency department. She shared her frustration over her psychiatrist's inability to get her mood swings under control. Her medication dosage had been increased until she became toxic. Then the dose was lowered. No matter what her psychiatrist did, she continued having radical mood swings and thoughts of hopelessness which led to thoughts of killing herself.

We hit the freeway and I got a set of vitals. Scanning the hospital face sheet, I noticed she was a Christian. "Sharon... I have a stupid question for you."

"What's your question?"

"Could you ever imagine yourself being healed of bi-polar disorder?"
There was a long pause.

"Well... I'm not sure. I mean... yeah, I want to be healed of it. I'm sick and tired of living like this. But it seems like there isn't any hope for that."

I thought about her answer for a few minutes. I wasn't sure if I should just ask if I could pray with her or go a little deeper. "Umm... I have another stupid question for you," I said hesitantly.

She looked at me. "Are these questions going somewhere?"

It wasn't the answer I was hoping for. But she didn't tell me to buzz off, either. I sensed that she wanted to talk, but she didn't understand where it was all leading and that made her uncomfortable. It was time to show my cards.

"Yeah, the questions are going somewhere. I'm trying to find out if you want to be healed of bi-polar, because I think you can be. I've been praying with my patients for a few years now, and I see a lot of them healed. They've been healed of all kinds of things like neck and back pain and migraines. I'll admit I haven't seen a lot of people healed of mental illness yet, but I've been asking God to teach me how to do it... and I was hoping I could pray for you."

"I'm a Christian," she said matter-of-factly.

"I know you are."

"No... I really am," she insisted.

"Yeah, I know you are. That's what it says on the hospital face sheet. And hardly anyone lies about that when they register." I held up the face sheet and pointed to the word "Christian" under religious preference.

"So what are you?" She asked.

"I'm a Christian, too."

"Are you really?" She let out a sigh of relief. "Oh thank God. I was dreading even asking you because I just knew you were going to be a Mormon."

"Nope... definitely not a Mormon. Just your average Jesus freak who likes to pray with people," I said with a smile.

"This is too weird," she began. "Last night before I came to the hospital, I told God I can't do this anymore. I'm at the end of my rope. This crap has to end one way or the other. I've been dealing with it for more than 20 years and I can't take it anymore. I asked God to do something about it... and then you show up and ask if I want to be healed."

I smiled. She cried. She finally knew where the stupid questions were going.

"How old were you when you were diagnosed with bi-polar?"

"I was twenty-one."

"I have another stupid question... "

She smiled.

"Was there any kind of emotionally traumatic event that happened in the year before you were diagnosed?"

"Yes. My mom died."

"How did she die?"

"She killed herself. She failed the first two times, but she got it right the third time. It was a few months later when I was diagnosed."

"That's what I thought. You know... I've been interviewing people about the onset of symptoms like bi-polar and fibromyalgia and it's surprising how often the symptoms begin shortly after an emotionally traumatic event."

"I first developed symptoms when I was seven. My mom was bi-polar, too. But no one else was allowed to have problems in our house. She got all the attention. It wasn't until after she died that my symptoms were officially diagnosed." She talked about what it was like growing up with a bi-polar mom. I wrote my report as I listened.

"Hey... maybe you're an angel!" She blurted out.

"I promise I'm not an angel. But I am a messenger from God. He sent me to tell you that He wants you healed. The question is... do you want to be healed? Now, think about it carefully, because if you do get healed your life is gonna change, big time. No more doctor appointments, no more medications, no more drama."

Another long, silent pause filled the ambulance.

"Look Sharon, I know this is kinda weird. I'm asking all these questions because I know that not everyone wants to be healed. I often ask people in wheelchairs if they wanted to be healed and sometimes they said no, because they're afraid that if they get healed, their disability checks will stop and they aren't sure they can find a job. Some people thrive on the drama that their condition causes. They get to be the center of attention and they grow accustomed to it. They know that if they get healed, the attention will stop and they aren't sure if they want that. A lot of people get something they need from their illness, so they don't really want it to leave. What I need to know from you is... are you ready for some changes? Because if God heals you, everything is going to change."

She tearfully took my hand. "I want to be healed, and I want you to pray with me."

I closed my eyes. "Holy Spirit, touch Sharon's heart and heal her mind and emotions. Erase the painful memories and establish her true identity as a child of God." In a vision, I saw her standing with a man, and felt like it represented her husband. "Lord, strengthen her marriage, destroy the enemy's work, and give her and her husband a renewed commitment to their marriage." I continued praying for a few minutes and then let her rest.

With tear-filled eyes she spoke once again. "There's no way you would know this, but my husband and I are separated. He filed for divorce. He just couldn't take it anymore."

We talked about her marriage and I encouraged her not to give up on it. "If you get healed of bi-polar, it may bring healing to your marriage."

"What if I don't get healed?" She asked.

"What if you do?" I replied. "Sharon, not every healing is immediate. A few people I've prayed for felt heat or tingling when I prayed and their healing came in a matter of seconds. But it doesn't always work that way. For a lot of people, it took ten or fifteen minutes before they realized they were healed. For some, it was the next day and for others it was three or four days later.

Just because you don't feel a bolt of electricity going through you, it doesn't mean you're not healed. I believe you are healed and the best thing you can do is to believe it too, and start living as if you aren't bi-polar anymore."

"It's been so long. More than 20 years. I'm not even sure how I would live if I wasn't bi-polar. I even have an 'I'm bi-polar' t-shirt," she said with a smile.

"Sharon, the illness is not your identity. Your identity is not a bi-polar person. You're a child of the King of Heaven and you happen to have a condition. But the condition is not who you are. You need to start seeing yourself differently. You are a daughter of the Most High God. That's your identity."

She smiled. "I need to remember that."

We pulled into the hospital parking lot. The journey had come to an end. We wheeled her inside and got her registered. After she hopped off the gurney, she gave me and my partner a hug. We exchanged a few last words as the nurse looked on.

"Are we done with our little love-fest yet?" The nurse asked impatiently.

I gave a quick report to the nurse and got her signature, then handed Sharon her lunch. It was time to clean the gurney and get a cup of coffee. My job isn't perfect, but there are some days when I really love it to pieces.

Tacos, Margaritas & Torn Biceps

ONE OF MY MORE RECENT EMT partners and I had been working together for about six months. He was ten years younger than me, single, and not affiliated with any religion that I knew of. Although he believed in God, he'd never been taught any specific beliefs about who God was or what He was like. My partner had led a colorful life, working different jobs including a job connected to the pornography industry, spending time in jail for petty crimes, and drifting aimlessly through life, until six years ago when he became an EMT.

The uniform he now wears did something to reform his self-image. He used to see himself as a troublemaker, but now he sees himself as a contributor to the good of society. And that's a stretch for a guy who has a massive problem with an orphan spirit and a deeply rooted sense of rejection and inadequacy. My partner is adopted. His parents did the best they could to raise him, but I'm guessing they didn't have the tools to give him the right identity. So God arranged for me to be his mentor for a while. And that's kinda what my life had been like for the year he and I were partners. My assignment was trying to teach a forty-something year old guy who God made him to be. If I'm to be perfectly honest, it was one of the most frustrating things I've ever been through. He pushed my buttons nearly every day and most of the time, he wasn't aware he was doing it.

If you're not familiar with the term *orphan spirit,* I'll give you a brief description of what it is and why it's such a problem. A few years ago, I had a dream where Bill and Benny Johnson discerned that the orphan spirit was the greatest problem in the church today. Like all evil spirits, the orphan spirit works in our lives through lies and deception. An evil spirit has the ability to influence you only to the degree that you believe its lies. If you reject its lies, it is powerless against you. If you accept its lies, it will be able to influence you in some way. The particular lie that the orphan spirit sells is the idea that you're on your own and that no one is going to take care of you. It denies that God is a loving Father who is able to provide for your needs. When you meet someone who acts as if they must provide for themselves, and never expects anyone to help them, you've found someone who is living under the influence of an orphan spirit. And that description fit my partner to a tee.

My partner had a habit of complaining about the price of just about everything. If he could get a refill on soda at one gas station for a dollar, he'd complain when he went to another gas station and had to pay fifty cents more. If a bag of chips was $1.59 at one place and $2.00 somewhere else, he'd whine about having to pay too much. I found it amusing at first, but after a while, it hit me. Here's a guy who is living paycheck to paycheck, in a job that pays a little more than minimum wage, and he's just trying to stay out of debt. When you've had to pay your own way for everything you've ever had, money can be a big deal. It dawned on me one day that no one had ever shown him what real generosity looked like. So I figured it was up to me to teach him something about it.

We had a ritual of stopping at the Circle K to get coffee every morning. A couple of weeks after we began working together, I began paying for his coffee or soda. He liked that and he allowed me to do it for a while with no complaints. Then I started buying him breakfast or lunch once in a while. He didn't complain about that either. I could tell he was grateful. Then one day, he got to the counter before me and paid for my coffee. I thanked him and we left. I didn't make a big deal of it outwardly, but on the inside, I was glowing. The plan was working.

As the weeks went on, the buying-for-your-partner thing escalated and he was now buying me lunch too. And he did it with a smile on his face. It wasn't like he was doing it to prove a point or doing it grudgingly. I could tell that he sincerely liked showing generosity toward me. Something was changing inside him.

One day my partner hurt himself while lifting a heavy patient. Some of the people we transport weigh between 500 and 600 pounds (200 to 300 kilos). The injury appeared to be a partially torn right bicep. Every time he flexed his forearm, he had a sharp pain in his upper arm.

He's a macho type of guy who doesn't want to appear to be a sissy and he refused to see a doctor. But day after day, every time he lifted the gurney with a heavy patient, I could see his pain.

I had a real problem with praying for him to be healed. He'd heard a few patients thank me for praying with them when we dropped them off at the hospital, but he had no clue what I'd been doing for the last five years and I wanted to keep it that way. Now that might sound strange to some of you, so let me explain:

I have a lot of friends who read my stories. Most of them are friends from social networks, but almost none of them are co-workers. If you work with me, your chances of connecting with me on one of my social networks is just about zero. I'm pretty deliberate about keeping my online life and my workplace life separate. My co-workers don't know who "Praying Medic" is. When a co-worker sees me praying with someone at work, they think I'm just another person who happens to pray for people. They don't know the things you know about me. God has allowed me to remain anonymous on the internet and at work, and I'm happy to keep things that way, at least for now. So I was trying not to blow my cover, but how was I supposed to keep a lid on things when my partner had a torn bicep and refused to see a doctor?

One day, while we were at a hospital, I got up the nerve to ask if I could try to get him healed. He said, "Sure."

I placed my hand on his upper arm. "Bicep, be healed. Spirit of pain, leave now." I asked if he felt anything.

"It tingles a little and it feels warm."

"Does it still hurt?"

He flexed at the elbow. "Yeah, it still hurts."

I placed my hand on his arm again. "Lord, bring your presence. Bicep, I command you to be healed. Pain and inflammation, leave now." I asked him to test it again.

"I feel tingling and heat, but it still hurts."

"I think you'll notice that the pain will gradually go away." The next day at work he didn't notice any difference in the level of pain. Nothing had changed. As the weeks passed, it seemed as though maybe his arm was getting better, little by little, but there was nothing dramatic happening.

The week that I returned from vacation, we transported a lot of larger than average patients. I went home several nights that week with back pain and had to lie on an ice pack. On one of these transports, my partner injured his other arm. He had the same symptoms again, pain in his upper arm when he flexed at the elbow. But this time it seemed worse. It looked like he tore his left bicep, but he also couldn't raise his arm or extend it straight out without having severe pain. I wondered if he didn't also have a partially torn rotator cuff. There was no way to tell, because he still refused to be seen by a doctor.

My partner seems to have been treated harshly over the years whenever he said or did something wrong. I noticed that when he took us to a wrong address he was a lot harder on himself than I would have been. To me, it's no big deal when you start a new job to make a few mistakes. But he beat himself up verbally when he messed up and I sensed it was because of how people had treated him in the past. I decided to give him a lot of grace for making mistakes, which isn't always easy for me.

I've always had a problem dealing with people who can't do their job competently. So I had to ask God to give me more than the usual amount of patience with him as he learned the ropes. I bit my tongue often when he took a wrong turn or said something that would have normally caused me to correct him. In fact, my correction of him was one of the biggest issues I had to deal with. There are things you have to know and things you must do to not hurt patients in EMS, but a lot of the things we say and do are not important enough to warrant correction. And most of his mistakes were little ones that didn't really matter. I tried to let most of them slide, but as time went on it became more difficult.

We have what I call a little resort in our back yard. When my wife asked me to move to Arizona, the only thing I required our home to have was a swimming pool. The majority of our back yard is taken up by a large, free-form diving pool, surrounded by potted flowers and palm trees, making it a great place to relax after work. In the summer, we often make tacos and margaritas and enjoy them as we watch the sunset from our lounge chairs next to the pool. When my partner asked what I had planned after a long day at work, I'd often tell him I was going home, making tacos and margaritas, and sitting by the pool. I did it often enough that it became a running joke between us.

The day he injured his left arm, it just happened that we had a repairman coming to fix our furnace, which decided to stop working a few days before the first cold spell of the year. Because we only have one car, and my wife had to be home while the repairman was fixing the furnace, I had to ask my partner to give me a ride home. When

I asked if he could give me a ride, he said he would, with one condition: we had to make tacos and margaritas for him. I called my wife. She said she'd be happy to get things started.

When I got home, there was a chopped onion sautéing in my favorite frying pan. I added some minced garlic and the rest of the stuff for the tacos, then put some crushed ice in the blender and made a pitcher of margaritas. The dinner was great. We talked about the day we had at work and how he injured his arm. I thought to myself as we talked that it would be the perfect time to get him healed. As we sat at the table, sipping our drinks, I told my wife we ought to pray for him and see if we could get his arm healed. He was willing to let us give it a shot. I told him about some of the people we'd seen healed and my wife shared the story about the Kirby vacuum salesman.

My wife and I placed our hands on his left arm. She prayed in tongues, I commanded the pain to leave and spoke to the muscle, tendons, cartilage and connective tissue, telling them to be healed. He said his upper arm suddenly felt numb. No tingling and no heat, just a weird numbness that wasn't there before. He still felt some pain when he flexed his arm, so we kept praying. I commanded spirits of pain to leave and commanded the bicep to be healed. My wife kept praying in tongues. He noticed that the severity of pain decreased each time we prayed, so we kept praying for about ten minutes.

At this point, I felt as if we'd made pretty decent progress and I believed the healing would continue during the night. He was grateful for the improvement we'd made, but he had to leave to take care of a little crisis involving a friend who called him during dinner. I thanked him for giving me a ride home and told him I'd see him in the morning at work.

The next day at work, we had the usual number of calls. I didn't notice anything different about the way he was lifting and he didn't say anything to indicate that he was healed. A couple of hours before the end of shift, he looked at me with a smile. He showed me that he could raise his arm up and flex it with almost no discomfort. He said he'd been trying to figure out all day a logical explanation for why his arm was feeling so much better. He wanted to rule out natural explanations before acknowledging a supernatural one.

"I remembered I took a bunch of supplements yesterday morning and I thought maybe that was what happened."

"Do you think that's the real reason you feel better?"

"No. I did some research on the stuff I took and none of it would have made my arm better." He smiled and grew quiet. We both knew the real reason behind the healing.

A few days later, he still had good range of motion. He had a little pain when he put his arm in a strange position like reaching behind the seat to put his seat belt on, but I put his healing at around 90 percent. He told me his right bicep was also healed. It took a long time, but the pain was mostly gone and he put it at about the same stage of healing as the left one. I have no explanation as to why one bicep would take over a month to heal and the other one manifested healing in 24 hours. I spent a few more months working with him. There were a lot more lessons we both needed to learn.

Bell Rock

We had been entertaining guests for a few weeks in November, including my friend David McLain. He needed a vacation and I needed some company, so he flew to Phoenix for six days to catch up on what we've been doing. Also in town were my stepson and his wife. They happened to be visiting as part of their honeymoon. We'd also been entertaining my editor, Lydia Blain. We all planned to take a day trip to the Grand Canyon, but McLain brought with him the kind of weather we seldom see in Arizona—four straight days of cool, cloudy, rainy weather. We joked about his angels bringing the atmosphere of the Northwest to our region, but that's another story. Since near freezing temperatures and snow were in the forecast for the Grand Canyon, we decided to aim for a different destination: Sedona. Situated at a lower elevation, the threat of snow was less likely and the women in the group liked the idea of shopping in the downtown galleries and boutiques Sedona is known for.

The Sedona area is famous for another feature—four energy portals that are frequented by curious seekers looking for spiritual adventures. (An energy portal is a kind of spiritual gateway to the supernatural realm.) On the way to Sedona, McLain kept in contact with a couple of friends who suggested we ask the Holy Spirit if He had any assignments for us in Sedona. We felt as though He did. The assignment involved freeing a couple of angels who seemed to be bound by the enemy in the portal system. After discussing it and praying, we felt our task was to set the angels free and allow them to continue with their assignments. (If you're wondering how an angel of God could be trapped inside a portal by the enemy, consider the fact that the angel that was sent to deliver a message to Daniel was detained by the enemy for 21 days.)

I think it's a dangerous policy to pick fights with spiritual powers when you don't have a clear and confirmed assignment from God against them. There are thousands of spiritual bad guys out there in every state and nation of the world that you could pick a fight with simply because they're on the other team. I don't make a habit of picking fights, mostly because I've learned from people who have picked fights that it's a good way to get your head kicked in. When you go up against spiritual powers you're not assigned to battle, or equipped to handle, you're probably going to take a beating.

I agreed to get involved in this operation for several reasons: The first was that, as a resident of Arizona, I represent God's government in this region. I'm not exactly sure how far my governmental authority extends beyond Arizona, but I'm confident it covers the geographic area of my state. We received confirmation from two trusted prophetic friends who live outside the region who were not in contact with each other about what was going on inside the portal. I had McLain along, and he'd been involved in this kind of thing before. I personally invited him as a representative of my region, which allowed him to operate under my authority as a local representative. I also invited a few dozen prayer warriors to cover us in prayer, though I didn't tell them what we were up to. I would advise anyone to put a little thought, a lot of caution, and some serious prayer into your plans if you ever decide to try something like this.

After spending a few hours shopping in town, we headed to Bell Rock, the location of the largest energy portal. McLain and I believe that the portals were created by God, but we consider them now to be under the control of the kingdom of darkness. We decided to keep at a safe distance while we engaged in a little warfare. We found a public parking area about a half mile away and surveyed Bell Rock and the much larger Courthouse Butte that dwarfed it, standing a few hundred yards to the northeast. We quickly and quietly spoke our decrees of freedom over the portal.

As soon as I began speaking, I sensed a strong presence of God's glory being released. With my eyes closed, I saw a thick cover of dark clouds in the spirit that were pierced by a shaft of light. An opening appeared in the clouds that gave way to a small hole of blue sky overhead. I saw lightning strikes coming from the clouds above and a release of gold dust into what appeared to be the portal itself. It was all very interesting to watch. The prayers and commands only took a few minutes. After we did our thing from the parking lot, we decided to go in for a closer look.

We parked at the visitor center and hiked the trail to the base of Bell Rock. We talked about many things during our walk. I gave our friends a botany lesson on the cacti, agave, and yucca plants that surrounded us. We took a lot of photos and marveled at God's creation. I have a real fondness for the red rocks of Sedona and for the people who live here. I feel as though one day, God might open a door for us to teach the spiritually hungry souls who come here about the one true light they're looking for—Jesus.

Bell Rock – Healing at the Circle K

AFTER LEAVING BELL ROCK, CONTENT that the enemy had been dealt with and the angels had been freed, we drove south to the little town of Oak Creek. The parking lot at Bell Rock is less than a mile from a Circle K gas station. The car needed gas, the crew needed food, and I needed coffee for the long drive home. And as you know, Circle K is my favorite coffee stop. McLain hopped out of the car and swiped his credit card to pay for the gas. I was too tired to argue with him. He shoved the pump nozzle in the tank with a smile. I adjusted my sunglasses, gave him a grin and went inside.

After grabbing a bottle of water for my wife, I filled my travel mug halfway with hazelnut creamer and topped it off with coffee. I waited in line at the counter while my wife waited in line for the bathroom. I noticed a massive Reese's Peanut Butter Cup package at the counter and I picked it up to examine it closer. It was a two-pack of peanut butter cups. Each peanut butter cup weighed eight ounces. I held it up so my wife could see it. "Hey baby... want me to get this for you?" She gave me a sarcastic look so I put it back on the shelf. The woman behind the counter asked if I was going to buy it. "Nope. Just the coffee refill and a bottle of water. The Reese's thing is an inside joke."

"Really? Tell me more."

"About two months ago we were shopping at Costco when the cart suddenly made a turn down the candy aisle without my consent. No... honest. It really did! So we're cruising' past all the Costco-sized packages of chocolate and suddenly my wife says, 'Hey honey... I'd kinda like that bag of chocolate peanut butter cups, if you don't mind.' She batted her eyelashes at me, so I hoisted the three and a half pound bag from the shelf and tossed it in the cart. Over the next three weeks, we slowly devoured the peanut butter cups and during that time, she developed an excruciating case of pain and tenderness all over her body. I couldn't touch her anywhere without hurting her. Every time she tried to pick something up off the floor she had pain. So check this out… about three days after the peanut butter cups are gone, her pain left. I mentioned it to her one day and her jaw nearly hit the floor. She had no pain before we bought the peanut butter cups and the pain suddenly ended when they were gone. The pain was caused by the sudden increase in sugar. We've known for years that there's a connection between sugar intake and chronic pain caused by inflammation. But we'd never seen such obvious evidence of it. So the thing with the peanut butter cups was just our little inside joke."

So after I explained all this, the clerk began asking me questions about chronic pain. Like the pain she had in her knee.

(Cue spooky music.)

I asked her about the pain and let her tell me as much as she was comfortable sharing. "Would you like to be healed?" I asked.

"I sure would. Are you a healer?"

"I sure am."

Now you need to remember the setting of this encounter. Sedona is the New Age capitol of North America. They have more energy healers living there than the Mayo clinic has doctors. So it was no surprise for a stranger to offer healing at a gas station. People who are seeking the supernatural come there for a reason. They all work different jobs, mostly in the town's tourism industry. But nearly everyone who lives in Sedona comes there seeking an encounter with the supernatural. What they really need of course, is a radical encounter with the Holy Spirit and the kingdom of God.

So I got down on my knees and felt both of her knees. Her left knee was much more swollen than her right one. "You don't have arthritis, do you?" I asked. She told me about the tests her doctors had done and what treatments she'd been through. Most of the swelling was fluid that had collected in the joint over time. I placed my hands around her knee. "Spirits of pain and inflammation, I command you to leave in the name of Jesus. Swelling, leave. Cartilage, bones, tendons, muscles, nerves and ligaments, be healed." I asked what she felt.

"My whole knee feels really warm."

"Well… it looks like you're being healed." Now it was my turn to use the bathroom.

While I was away, McLain, who had been watching the whole thing go down, gave the woman some advice. "If the pain ever comes back, tell God, 'whatever you did to heal my knee, keep doing it'." When I came out of the bathroom the woman said, "Now it's tingling all over."

I told her, "Tingling is good. That means you're being healed." I paid for the coffee and the bottle of water, smiled, shook her hand and left. McLain was waiting in the car with the rest of the crew. He told me what he said to her. I told him I like to leave people with a little instruction on how to keep their healing and I appreciated him giving her some advice. He said it was kinda comical watching the customers react to what I was doing. I wasn't aware that anyone was paying attention to me.

"Oh yeah. This one guy came in the store and when I asked if he wanted to get past me, he said, 'No, that's okay… I want to watch what this guy is doing.'" I guess even in a place like Sedona, things like this can draw a crowd.

We drove home and talked about many things. I got to teach him a little bit about healing, and he got to teach me how to do spiritual warfare without either of us becoming a casualty. All in all, it was an excellent outing.

Got Any Pain Pills?

I WAS HAVING ONE OF those days where I just wanted to leave work and go home. My patient was being demanding and his needy condition was getting on my nerves. I know I should have been more sympathetic to him. He's a quadriplegic who lived in a nursing home for years after a car accident left him paralyzed. This particular morning, his nurse found blood returning from his feeding tube, so we transported him to the hospital for what seemed like a GI bleed.

The nursing home was across the street from the hospital, making the transport time about two minutes. It's amazing how irritated I can get on such a short transport. On the way out the door he asked for a glass of water. His nurse was nice enough to send his cup of ice water along, but I'd set it on the back of the gurney and somehow it managed to tip over. The water was now all over the floor of the ambulance. I told him he'd have to wait a few minutes. Next, he wanted me to suction his tracheostomy. It didn't seem like it needed to be suctioned, but I suctioned him a couple of times as we left the nursing home. Before I had the suction equipment put away, he asked for a pain pill. That's when I lost it.

His demands had gotten the better of me and in a stern voice I said, "Look, I don't have any pain pills and we're going to be at the hospital in 30 seconds. I'd really appreciate it if you would just chill out for a few minutes until we get there."

Normally it takes a lot for someone to get on my nerves, but today, for some reason, I was unusually irritable. My partner must have heard me and knew I was pretty ticked off. When we were through with the call, he drove across the street to a restaurant he knows I like. "You look like you need lunch," he said.

He was right. I was hungry, so I thanked him and when the ambulance came to a stop, I hopped out. As I walked to the entrance of the restaurant, a stranger walked up to me and asked, "Hey man, you don't have a pain pill do you?"

Wondering if it was some kind of cruel joke, I just looked at him for a minute in stunned silence. I thought to myself, in what world do you walk up to a paramedic in a parking lot and ask for a pain pill?

Then another thought came to mind. Maybe this was a divine set-up. Maybe it was an opportunity to get this guy healed. "Why do you want a pain pill?" I asked.

"I broke my leg in two places. It was an on the job injury. They did surgery, but it didn't go well." He pulled up his pant leg and showed me the scars near his calf and ankle. He now lives in constant pain.

After checking out his leg I said, "Why don't we go inside."

Once we were inside the restaurant, I got in line to order some food. He stayed near the door, looking around like he was waiting for someone. After I ordered my food, I went back and asked him, "Would you like to be healed?"

He said, "Sure."

"I'm going to pray over your leg." I knelt beside him and placed my hand on his leg, just above the ankle. "Ligaments, bones, muscles, tendons and nerves, be healed in the name of Jesus. Do you feel anything?"

"Yeah. My lower leg feels warm."

I continued praying then I asked him to test it out. He walked around the lobby for a while and said it felt better, but there was still some pain. I placed my hand on his lower leg and repeated the process. Once again he tested it out, and again he said it was better, but there was still a little pain remaining. I prayed a third time and afterward, he said, "It feels really good now. The pain is almost gone."

People in the restaurant were looking at us, including a woman who seemed more interested than everyone else. I looked at her and said, "What are you smiling at?"

"If you're through praying for my husband, will you pray for me next?"

As I approached, I put my arm around her shoulder. "And what do you need prayer for?"

"I'm seeing my doctor tomorrow to have a hysterectomy. They found cancer and I'm really scared."

160

I placed my hands on her shoulders. "Holy Spirit, bring your presence." I felt His glory arrive and noticed that she was starting to sway back and forth. "Are you feeling anything?"

"Just a wave of peace washing over me."

"Cancer, I command you to leave in the mighty name of Jesus. Lord, I bless your work of healing in her body. Sickness and disease, get out now." When I was done praying she gave me a warm hug.

"Thank you so much," she said. Her husband shook my hand, unable to say anything. He just smiled from ear to ear. I picked up my food and headed for the door.

Somehow, all the irritation I felt a few minutes earlier was gone. People ask for pain pills because they're in pain. Jesus sent us into the world to take away the pain and suffering of mankind. Not with pills, but with power. He also sent us as messengers of peace. Maybe I need to learn how to live from the peace of His presence more often. God knows I could use a little more peace.

Nothing to Worry About

WE STOPPED AT THE NURSE'S station to pick up the paperwork and get report on our patient. As she handed me the envelope, the nurse said, "She's really nervous about the procedure, so I hope you're ready for a challenge this morning. And there's a little problem... she wasn't supposed to eat anything, but there wasn't an actual order saying that, so she had two cans of soda this morning, but nothing for breakfast. If you'd pass that along, I'd appreciate it."

I opened the envelope and flipped through the paperwork, looking for a face sheet so I could get her biographic information entered in my computer. "What's she going in for?"

"She's having a bronchoscopy because she's been whistling when she breathes and they want to see if there's an obstruction somewhere. She had an accident riding a horse about a month ago and has a skull fracture with a cerebral hematoma. After the accident, she was in a coma for 11 days and had respiratory failure with a tracheostomy that's capped now. All things considered, she's actually in pretty good shape. She can walk and talk and is alert. Oh... and I gave her a milligram of Ativan to calm her down a little."

"Did you save any for me?"

"Do your best to keep her calm, okay? She's really anxious."

"Nervous Nellies are my specialty. I'll make sure she knows she has nothing to worry about."

We pushed the gurney to her room and my partner went in. I stayed out in the hallway to enter her name, date of birth, address and phone number in the computer. After I finished, I walked into her room.

Looking her in the eye, I said in my best game show host voice, "I just want to let you know you have nothing to worry about!"

She busted up laughing. So did her mom, who was standing next to her bed. "So the nurse must have told you... " she said, laughing.

"They tell us everything... oh, wait... maybe I should introduce myself." We got the introductions out of the way, and I asked if she had any questions.

"Yeah, I do have a question. Exactly what are they going to do to me?"

"Didn't anyone tell you?"

"Not really. They just said I'm going to have a bronchoscopy and I'm not sure what that is."

"If no one told you what's going to happen, I can see why you're anxious about it, so let me explain." Sahara had a tracheostomy that was capped, because she was able to breathe on her own. "The procedure you're having done is called a bronchoscopy, where they take a small fiber-optic camera and feed it into your trachea. They're going to look around, to see if there's anything wrong."

"Am I going to be awake when they do it? I swear I'll freak out if I am."

"Ha ha... good question. Umm... no, you're not going to be awake. They'll give you some happy juice to put you in la-la land so you won't remember a thing."

"Well that's good to know, because I do NOT want to be awake for it. Wait! Are they gonna stick any needles in me?"

"Well... yes, they will need to start an IV so they can give you the medicine to sedate you."

"I HATE needles! Isn't there any way they can do it without sticking me with a needle?"

"Look Sahara, they don't have to use a big needle. They'll probably use a small one. Don't worry, it won't hurt much."

"What if I'm not really in la-la land when they do it, and I'm actually awake but they don't know it? I don't want to feel anything."

"Sahara, here's what you need to do. When we get you to the hospital, you need to talk to the nurses and tell them your concerns. Ask them every question you can think of. Tell them what you're concerned about and make them answer all your questions. Let them know they aren't doing the procedure until you're comfortable with their answers. Does that sound like a plan you can live with?"

"Yeah, I can do that."

"Okay, well why don't we get you in the ambulance?"

Her mother asked if she could ride along with us. I said she could. We went to the ambulance, got her loaded and began the 30-minute drive to the hospital. I got my report started and let Sahara and her mother talk for a while. Eventually, I had to write down her chief complaint and I didn't actually know what that was yet.

"Sahara, what's bothering you the most right now?"

"The back of my head. If feels like someone is stabbing me with a knife over and over."

"Stabbing you with a knife?"

"Yeah." She pointed to the back of her head. "Right here. It's really sore all the time. I have these constant stabbing pains that won't go away."

"On a scale from one to ten how bad is the pain?"

"About a nine."

"How long have you had the stabbing pain?"

"I think I've had it ever since I came out of the coma."

"So... like a few weeks?"

"Yeah, I guess so."

If I were able to see in the spirit with the ease that some of my friends do, I would have expected to see some kind of demon standing behind her, holding a long metal blade, repeatedly jabbing it into her head. While I do sometimes see things that indicate the presence of demons, they aren't usually very dramatic.

We arrived at the place in our provider-patient relationship where a decision had to be made. I'd built a strong enough bridge with Sahara that she would probably trust me if I asked her about prayer. But the easy way out would be to let her continue talking with her mother the rest of the trip, while I finished my report. The thing is, I really wanted that pain in her head to stop. I felt a bit of confidence rising up inside of me as I looked at the back of her head. I knew that if I could just touch her, she would be healed. "I have a weird question for you Sahara."

"And what would that be?" She asked innocently.

"Can I pray for you?"

"Of course you can!" She said excitedly. Her mother smiled with approval.

"Okay. I'm going to place my hand... "

"Don't touch it!" She said fearfully. "It's really sensitive there."

"Alright, Sahara. I know it hurts. I'm not going to touch your head. How about if I hold my hand a couple inches away from the sore spot?"

"That's fine."

"Cool. I'd like tell you a story about someone who was healed last week." I shared a story about a young woman I prayed with who was healed of scoliosis. As I told the story, I held my hand a few inches from the back of her head.

"Sahara, do you feel any different?"

"No."

I was hoping that just sharing the testimony would release healing, but it didn't seem to do anything. It was time to get serious. "I command spirits of pain to leave right now, in the name of Jesus. I command soft tissue to be healed, I command bone to be healed, I command spirits of trauma to leave. Holy Spirit, bring your power upon this young lady and bless her with healing. Okay, what do you feel now?"

"Nothing," she said with a stunned look on her face. "I mean... there isn't any pain at all. It's completely gone. How did you do that?"

She felt the back of her head where the pain had been, gently at first, testing it to see if she could make it return, but it would not come back. She was healed, and she was pretty ecstatic about it. The look on her face was absolutely priceless and it made me laugh. "How great is God, Sahara?"

Her mother chimed in. "Sahara, when you were little, I remember you would sit in the front of the TV and watch Veggie Tales and sing that song, 'How Great is Our God?' You'd sing it over and over and over. You just loved that song."

Sahara and her mother continued their conversation and I went back to writing my report. And God... well, He's still out there doing what He does best. Healing hurt people and loving on them like the awesome Father that He is.

Healing the Past

YOU MAY HAVE NOTICED IN some of the previous stories that I'd been experiencing increasing problems with anger. The day before I went on this call, I spent two hours on the phone with a friend who took me through the process of being healed of emotional trauma that happened when I was a teenager. The trauma was connected to the anger. The day after I received my healing, I went on a call to an Emergency Department to transport a young woman for mental health treatment. We arrived early and as I waited for her to be ready for the transport, I read the transcript dictated by the social worker who interviewed her. Her depression and suicidal thoughts began a year and a half earlier after she had her child. She suffered from postpartum depression that never went away. Since her child had been born, she had several outbursts of extreme anger. In one incident she punched holes through the wall of her apartment. In another incident she almost stabbed her husband with a knife. She had come to the hospital this time for treatment of depression and suicidal thoughts brought on by another incident with her husband where she was overcome by feelings of anger and tried to push him into traffic. I also read where she said she had been molested as a teenager.

As I read her report, it became obvious that she was suffering from the same thing I had just been healed of. It seemed like she had a wounded (or fragmented) soul that was temporarily taking control of her during certain events and she was overreacting to the situation in anger. We loaded her in the ambulance and I spent the first ten minutes telling her about my own struggles with anger and how I had been healed the day before by talking with a friend. She listened intently and I could that tell my testimony was giving her hope. "I know you were molested as a teenager," I said. "Do you want him to die?"

"I don't want him to die a violent death. I just want him to die and go away."

"My friend got me healed of my own problems with anger and I think we can get you healed. The first thing I did was go back to one of the events where I could feel the anger. Then my friend led me in a few prayers. When we were done, he had me go back again and try to feel the anger from the events, but I couldn't feel it any more. It was like there was a door that I could go through any time I wanted to and could relive the experiences and feel the anger again. But after we were done, it was like the door had been closed. In fact, I couldn't even find the door. So here's my question: Would you like to be healed of your anger?"

"Yes I would." She put out her hand and I took hold of it.

"I need you to go back in your mind to one of the incidents that created a feeling of anger. When you can feel it, let me know."

It only took a few seconds. "Okay, I feel it."

"I'm going to have you repeat what I say." These are the prayers we said together:

"God, I confess my anger as sin."

"Jesus, I believe you died to take away my sins."

"I do not want to be controlled by anger anymore."

"Lord, I ask you to take this anger from me and give me your peace in return."

"I ask you to heal the wounds in my soul caused by anger and I receive your healing."

She repeated everything I said. "Okay, now I want you to go back and try to feel the emotions from any of the events." She sat there for a moment then looked at me in shock.

"Crazy, huh? You can't feel the anger any more, can you?"

She immediately realized she was healed and her mind was already thinking about how this could be used for other problems. "Do you think it would work for other emotions?"

"Like what?"

"Sadness."

"I think it will work for any emotion that you don't want. God will often give you something in exchange for what you give Him. So if you give Him your sadness, He may give you His joy in return. If you give Him your feelings of rejection, He may give you His acceptance. This is something you can do yourself. I mean, you're going to be sitting here for a couple of days with not much to do. You may want to sit quietly and talk with God and ask Him to heal of all this stuff."

We arrived at the hospital and got her registered. Before we left she thanked me for taking the time to help her. This was my first attempt at doing emotional healing with one of my patients and it seemed to be successful. The amazing thing is that it didn't take two hours, but only ten minutes.

I don't think emotional healing needs to be as hard or as complicated as some people make it out to be. It doesn't have to be a long process. I've used this approach dozens of times since this transport and the results have been better than I expected. With some people, their physical symptoms of pan have been healed along with their emotions. I have a friend who uses this process which he now calls the "one minute healing prayer." I realize that this approach may not work this well or this quickly for every person. Sometimes it will take longer, depending on the severity of the emotional trauma. I'm working on a book right now on the subjects of inner healing and deliverance. I'll share my own testimony of healing and many others in that book when it becomes available.

Unicorns Are Awesome and so Is Jesus

WE WERE EARLY FOR THE transport so I stopped at the nurse's station to get a report on our patient. Tracy was a 16-year-old girl who had spent the last three days in the hospital after trying to kill herself. We were transporting her to a mental health facility for evaluation and treatment. But there was just one problem. Tracy's mother was addicted to drugs and at the present time she was homeless. Before we could get her admitted to the receiving facility, her mother had to be there to sign her in. And with her being homeless, there was no guarantee she would be there. I've had to wait several hours for a parent or legal guardian to show up before a minor patient could be admitted, so when I hear that the parent's whereabouts are unknown, it always makes me a little uneasy.

I walked to her room and peeked inside and was surprised to find my partner already joking around with her. I watched them for a few minutes then introduced myself. Tracy's long hair was a layered with deep red and electric pink. The pink was the same color as the stuffed unicorn she clutched in her hands.

We talked for a while and as I got to know more about her, I took an instant liking to her. She reminded me of my daughter; happy, smiling often, and full of life. She didn't seem like the type of person who would be depressed or suicidal. It was time to leave, so I told her to get her personal belongings together. Holding up her cell phone and her unicorn, she said, "This is all I have. I'm ready."

I looked at the unicorn, then at her and said, "Unicorns are awesome. And you're awesome... therefore you are a unicorn." She busted up laughing and I helped her to the gurney. The trip would take about 30 minutes. I got a set of vitals and started asking about her medical history, prescription medications and allergies. She said she had scoliosis and was supposed to be taking a pain medication for it, but she didn't have a way to get the prescription filled.

"Scoliosis?" I asked. "How bad is your pain on a scale from one to ten?"

"About a seven most of the time. My back bones pop and make this crunching sound whenever I turn to the left or right."

I silently thought about my next move. I wondered if she'd be open to prayer and of course, I wondered if she'd actually be healed if I prayed with her. I decided to draw her into a deeper discussion by making her curious. "I have to tell you... I'm a little afraid you might be one of *those* people."

She turned to look at me. "One of *what* people?"

"One of those people I pray with who gets healed."

"What do you mean healed?"

"Well, I pray with a lot of my patients and some of them are healed. You have back pain and I'm pretty sure that if I prayed with you, it would be healed. Have you ever seen a healing miracle?"

"Yeah, once. When my gramma got sick and she lost the feeling in her left leg, the doctors said they would have to amputate it or else she would die. We all gathered around her and prayed and asked God to heal her. She got all the feeling back in her leg and they never did amputate it."

"Wow. That's pretty cool."

She looked at me. "I don't just have scoliosis," she said in a serious tone. "I have a problem in my knee, too." Pointing to her fibula and her tibia, she said, "There's nothing between these two bones in my leg. It's bone on bone. My knee hurts all the time."

"On a scale from one to ten how bad is the pain?"

"It's about a nine."

I sighed and looked at her. "Well, do you want to be healed or not?"

"Yeah. That would be cool."

I moved to a different seat in the ambulance so I could be next to her and explained what I was going to do. I placed my hand on her knee. "Spirits of pain, I command you to leave. Ligaments, tendons, bones, nerves and muscles, be healed."

Since the pad between the upper and lower bones of the leg is called the meniscus, and it seemed like her meniscus had deteriorated to where it was no longer doing its job, I commanded a new one to be created. "What do you feel?"

"Wow! It feels great!" She exclaimed.

"Go ahead, move it around. Test it out. I guarantee you, it's healed." She moved her leg and flexed her knee joint several times trying to make the pain return, but there was none. It was completely healed. "Are you ready to have your back healed?"

"Yes!" She said excitedly.

"Where's the pain?"

"In the middle, between my shoulder blades."

I placed my hand there. "Bones, come into alignment right now in the name of Jesus. Scoliosis, leave. Ligaments and nerves, be healed. What do you feel?"

"Heat." She said, grinning. "It feels really warm and it doesn't hurt anymore."

"Well that's because God is healing you."

I prayed again, but this time I spoke to her destiny. I declared God's identity over her and asked the Holy Spirit to remove painful emotions and memories and to heal her soul. I declared God's protection and provision. I figured a kid like her needed as much help as she could get. She became very relaxed and in a few minutes she was sleeping on the gurney with her unicorn clutched tightly to her chest. I let her sleep the rest of the way. My fears about her mom never materialized. She was waiting for us when we got there.

Unicorns are awesome... and so is Jesus.

THANK YOU FOR PURCHASING THIS BOOK

For inspiring articles and an up-to-date list of my books, go to my website, **PrayingMedic.com**.

Other books by **Praying Medic**

Divine Healing
Made Simple

Seeing in the Spirit
Made Simple

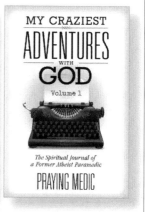

My Craziest Adventures
with God—Volume 1

A Kingdom View of
Economic Collapse

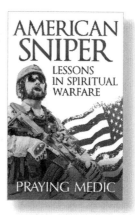

American Sniper:
Lessons in Spiritual Warfare

Made in the USA
San Bernardino, CA
20 October 2015